rry Keane has   in
eland and abroad. He grew up with the hills of the
urren and County Clare at his back door. As a geogra-
her he studied the area extensively and, together with
is walking and climbing, this gave him an intimate
amiliarity with these fascinating landscapes.

NEW IRISH WALKS AND SCRAMBLES 5

THE BURREN, ARAN ISLANDS AND COUNTY CLARE

by

Barry Keane

The Collins Press

Published in 1999 by
The Collins Press,
West Link Park,
Doughcloyne,
Wilton,
Cork,
Ireland

© Barry Keane 1999

British Library Cataloguing in Publication data.

A CIP catalogue record for this book is available from the British
Library.

Printed in Ireland by Colour Books Ltd.

Cover design by Upper Case Ltd, Cork

ISBN: 1-898256-83-7

CONTENTS

ACKNOWLEDGMENTS

I would like to thank Henry O'Keeffe without whom this book would not have been written. Indeed, his name would have appeared on the cover if he had not declined the recognition.

I would like to thank all the usual people involved in the series again for their assistance and suggestions. I would also like to mention the Geography, Archaeology and History Departments of UCC without whom my knowledge of Clare would have been much diminished. The late Dr Thorley Sweetman of the UCC Geology Department weaved his own special magic in the caves of the Burren, which will always remain places of great beauty for me.

The book could not be written without people giving me the time to do so and my mother and Caroline deserve a special mention for holding the fort at work on many days. Henry, Mairead, Louise and I toured all the side roads of Clare to ensure that the access to the routes was correct.

I would like to thank Andrea for typing the manuscript with her usual aplomb despite having to decipher my writing.

Finally thanks to Louise for everything.

To Louise
and my family

INTRODUCTION

This book is intended for walkers who wish to enjoy the freedom of the countryside. The easiest walks will take no more than one or two hours, while the longer walks will demand more planning. Each route description comes with its own sketch map, but the use of the new 1:50,000 Irish Ordnance Survey Discovery Series, which is an invaluable tool for any tourist in Ireland, is recommended. Please note that all placenames are spelled as they appear on the Discovery Maps. A useful companion to this walking guide is the field Guide, *Wild Plants of the Burren and the Aran Islands* by Charles Nelson.

COUNTY CLARE

Clare is one of the main tourist destinations in Ireland, especially its west coast. It is a county of great contrasts and a great place for walking, with layers of interest waiting to be peeled away at every turn.

Getting there: You can fly to Shannon Airport and this will put you within an hour of anywhere in the county. Alternatively, you can get the Iarnród Éireann train to Limerick or Galway, which will do the same thing. On Fridays, they run a train to Ennis, the county town, which makes life very easy for those using public transport. Bus Éireann runs services to all parts of the county, but some weekend timetabling can affect any plans you might have so be careful.

Accommodation: There is little or no problem getting accommodation at any standard from five-star hotels to private hostels and bunkhouses. Everything can be booked from the Irish Tourist Board (Bord Fáilte) with the exception of the hostels. However, they will give you information on all aspects of the county.

WALK GRADES:

Easy: These walks are generally short and chiefly on roads or forest tracks in National Parks, quite good for family groups, but everyone still needs to be kitted out for the weather. Many of these walks include sizeable villages en route to allow for a good break.

Moderate: These walks are longer and may well include some uphill climbing, still mostly on roads, but occasionally on tracks. These walks tend to take you further out into the countryside and there are a lot less opportunities for a break in a village along the way.

Difficult: These walks take you out on to open countryside or mountainside. You have to be reasonably fit and have a good idea of what you are up to. If you can use a compass so much the better, but you can follow much of these walks without one.

Very difficult: These are multi-day walks, which take a lot of planning, and a good degree of fitness to complete.

DISTANCES CONVERSION FROM METRIC TO IMPERIAL:
In the 1970s Ireland switched from Imperial measures to Metric. However, the conversion has neither been completed in people's minds, nor on the signposts around the country. This means that a lot of the time people will be converting back and forth between both measurement systems.

1 mile = 1760 yards = 1600 metres = 1.6 kilometres

HOW TO USE THE GUIDE:
Each route includes:
- A basic sketch map outlining the route.
- Route length and approximate time.
- The grade of the walk.
- A description of the journey to the start of the walk from Ennis, Limerick or Galway as appropriate and an Ordnance Survey map grid reference for the location.
- Parking details for the start of the route.
- A route description outlining the main features of the route.
- Mention of any archaeological, geomorphological or historical places of interest along the way.

EQUIPMENT
To go walking in the Irish countryside you should have a woollen cap and gloves, rain gear, food, a rucksack, map, solid walking boots with good ankle sup-

port, and two pairs of woollen socks. Do not wear jeans, cotton or nylon as these lose heat quickly and cause blisters.

ACCESS

The public has traditionally used the walks included in this book. Indeed many landowners do not object to people following traditional paths and tracks provided that users do not damage property, frighten livestock or abuse crops. It has to be pointed out, however, that a right-of-way may not exist in all cases and accordingly permission should be obtained from the landowner if in doubt. Respect the countryside, take the litter home and do not bring a dog where livestock might be encountered.

ROUTE 1
ENNISTIMON TO LEHINCH AND BACK

Map: OS Discovery Series Map No. 57
Distance: 8km
Grade: Easy
Average time: 1.5-2 hours
Getting there from Ennis: Take the N85 which branches off the N18 at the roundabout at the northern end of Ennis. Follow this road until you reach Ennistimon after 24km.
Parking: Park in the village where there is loads of parking on the main street. The start of the walk is at the signpost for Lehinch on the main street.
Starting point: Irish National Grid reference R131883

This walk is entirely on the road so it is no problem to anyone who is reasonably fit. Before you do anything else you will have to take a look at the falls in Ennistimon. From the Lehinch Junction go north up the main street on the left-hand side for a short distance to an archway on your left. Go through the archway and down the rather decrepit laneway to the falls which are impressive at any time, but especially after heavy rain. The underlying rock is shale and slate, and huge chunks of it have been washed away over the years to present the falls as they are now. Follow the river bank right downstream past the small electricity station and salmon ladder to the bottom of the falls for the best view.

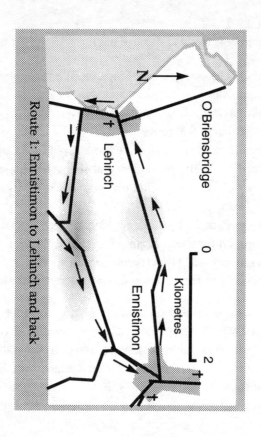

Return the way you came, back to the main street and go out the Lehinch road, which is unusual in rural Ireland in that it has a pavement and walkway along the side, making it easy for the walker. The first bridge you come to will give you a chance for another look at the falls from above (right side heading west), and then just trundle along the road towards Lehinch. As you go west the old track of the West Clare Railway runs along the side of the road. The railway was made famous by the songwriter Percy French in a song about its rather lax timekeeping. The author of songs like *The Mountains of Mourne* was sued by the train company over the song, but the lawsuit fizzled out when he countered with a claim for loss of earnings over the lateness of the train!

Continue along the road past the hospital on your left, and up the hill. You know that you are getting near the sea as the sand and marram grass begin to replace the inland grasses. From the top of the hill the view of the Atlantic opens out before you around to Liscannor bay and on towards the Cliffs of Moher. As you descend towards the village you pass ribbon development on your left and on the right, mostly holiday homes. Off to your right on the top of a hillock is a small ring fort which is reasonably well preserved considering its antiquity. This brings you into Lehinch and if you go straight on you will arrive down on to the beach. This is a lovely spot on a fine calm summer's day. However, it is not the safest beach in the world to go swimming from. If you have time you could walk north along the beach to the Inagh River outlet which blocks your path and east back to the road at O'Briensbridge. Then back south towards Lehinch along the side of the world famous golf links back into town past the FCA barracks.

After the beach with its *de rigeur* amusement arcade, go back into the town and south along the Milltown Malbay road past the church. Lunch is not a bad idea in any of the pubs, and some have reasonably good impromptu *ceilí* bands to pass an afternoon. At the end of the built-up area, go left and up the hill until you come to a T-junction after 1.5km. At the T-junction you might as well go right, considering you've climbed this far. This will bring you to a second T-junction after 200m and you go left here. The view west at this point is quite extensive and worth the little climb. At the next Y-junction take the left fork, and follow this road along for 2km back down to Ennistimon.

ROUTE 2
LISCANNOR TO THE CLIFFS OF MOHER AND BACK

Maps: OS Discovery Series Maps No. 57 and No. 51
Distance: 16km
Grade: Difficult
Average time: 4-5 hours walking time
Getting there from Ennis: Take the N85 which branches off the N18 at the roundabout at the northern end of Ennis. Follow this road until you reach Ennistimon after 24km. Take the first left in Ennistimon on to the N67 and go west to Lehinch 2km away. At Lehinch go right at the Garda station and north along the R478 Liscannor road past the golf links on your left. A sharp left at O'Briensbridge will bring you to Liscannor, 4km from Lehinch.
Parking: Park in the village where there is loads of parking on the main street. The start of the walk is at the phone box on the main street, just west of the independent hostel which is a goodplace to stay.
Starting point: Irish National Grid reference R065883

This is a long walk over mixed terrain with 200m of uphill. Still, the rewards more than compensate for the effort. From the famous McHugh's pub follow the signs south for the Burren Way which brings you to the coast in 200m. Follow the signs west past the old fort, and continue along the well-trodden track to the coast road. The views across Liscannor bay to Lehinch

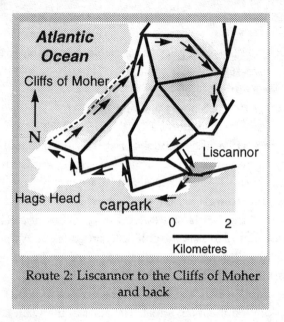

Route 2: Liscannor to the Cliffs of Moher
and back

and Miltown Malbay are very fine, but nothing in comparison to what's in store. Continue along past the carpark on your right as the coast and the road bend north. After 1km you come to a crossroads and you go left. Heading west you continue past the next turn on your right, and take the following one about 1.5km from the crossroads. Going north you soon come to a Y-junction and you go left here. All of this is on the Burren Way and there are little walking-man signs to help you. Continue uphill and out into the open countryside to the old signal tower on the coast and the start of the walk along one of Ireland's most spectacular pieces of scenery, the Cliffs of Moher.

The Cliffs of Moher are 200m high at their highest point, and you are now at the southern end of the cliffs. Basically, the soft shale and slate rock is overlain by a much harder sandstone which protects the upper section of the cliffs from weathering. As the Atlantic is busily ripping out the base, the cliffs retain their vertical profile due to the collapse of a higher section.

From here on you may need to take a few breaks along the coast as you are climbing 100m in 3km to the high point. As the cliffs weave in and out in a series of little headlands the view south gets better and better. You arrive at the visitor centre just under O'Brien's Tower where there is a shop, café and picnic tables. Whatever you do go north up the little track to O'Brien's Tower (a nineteenth-century folly, built as a viewing platform for the cliffs) as the view is excellent from here.

From the visitor centre go east through the carpark to the main road. If you are tired go right downhill along the R478 back to Liscannor, but it is more pleasant to head inland, and return to Liscannor on the back roads. To do this, go north along the main road towards Doolin for 1km (still on the Burren Way) around a sharp left-hand bend, and then sharp right down a third-class road to your right. Once down this take a sharp left after 200m which swings right almost immediately. Follow this road along the barren landscape with fine views north and south. Off to your left is Luogh Lough which is worth a look, but the road swings southward after 1km bringing you through the Ballycotteen hamlet and down through a sharp left bend followed by a sharp right after 100m, about 500m beyond Ballycotteen. The road joins up with another coming in from your right at a Y-junction and 200m east of this you come to a T- junction where you go right. Heading south you pass through another small cluster of houses (Ballycotteen South) and down to yet another T-junction at another cluster of houses. Go right downhill and at the next junction go right again past a couple of houses and west along the road. After 1km you will cross a bridge, Ballycotteen Bridge, over a small stream, and take the next left downhill and back to Liscannor 1km away.

Route 3

SLIEVECALLAN

Map: OS Discovery Series Map No. 57
Distance: 9km
Grade: Difficult
Average time: 3-4 hrs
Getting there from Ennis: Less than 50m on the southern side of the N85/N18 roundabout in Ennis take the R474 road west towards Miltown Malbay. This will take you past the golf course. Continue along this road through the village of Connolly after about 14km where you go left. Continue through The Hand Cross Roads after about 5km until you come to Drehidenagh Post Office on the right a further 3km farther on.
Parking: Park your car hereabouts making sure not to block any gates or obstruct traffic.
Starting point: Irish National Grid reference R113760

This is one of the more demanding walks in the guide, because it takes you out on to open mountainside with steep ground on many sides. It also means a 391m ascent, which sounds far more impressive as 1,300 feet. However, this is the finest vantage point in south Clare so this more than makes up for the effort.

From Drehidenagh Post Office walk west along the R474 to the next junction to the right. Go up this until it takes a sharp right after about 600m. Take the small third-class road to your left at this junction. This

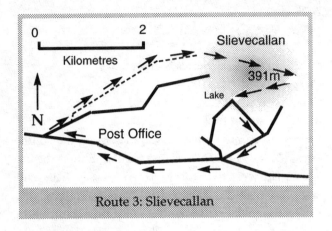

Route 3: Slievecallan

soon turns right again and degenerates into a mountain track. This will lead you to a stream which is the source of the Annagh River which enters the sea just south of the golf course at Spanish Point. Walk up the mountain following the stream, keeping the conifer plantations first on your left, then on your right. Just as the trees peter out around the 300m mark the route steepens quite a bit and you climb the next 30m in a short space of time. It levels off just as quickly and you find yourself on the broad top of Slieve Callan. The summit is approximately 800m from the top of the stream, and slightly south of east from there. If visibility is good you will have no problem in reaching the summit from the top of the stream. When weather is not good then you should use a compass to locate it.

If you don't have a compass then it is safer to return the way you came.

Once you reach the summit you will find the view extensive and worth the effort. From the summit cairn go south downhill. You will come to the top of the forestry in a short time (about 400-500m). When you get to the forestry go right. Continue westwards following the edge of the forest until you come to the track next to Lough Boolynagreana. Once on the track go left downhill past the stream coming out of the little lough, and up the slight rise ahead. At the next junction go right, around the bend and down the straight minor road to the main road. Once on the main road go right for 2km back to where you parked your car.

Route 4

Aillwee Cave and Mountain

Map: OS Discovery Series Map No. 51
Distance: 5km
Grade: Moderate
Average time: 2-3hrs
Getting there from Ennis: Leave Ennis by the N85, which branches off the N18 at the roundabout at the northern end of the town. After approximately 4km go right on to the R476 at Fountain Crossroads. This road will bring you to Corrofin after another 9km approximately. Go along the main street of the town towards Kilfenora, and past the Garda station on the left at the far end of town. Approximately 1km past the Garda station is Inchiquin Lough, which is worth a short detour down a track on the left. 3.5km beyond Corrofin you will come to Killinaboy with a couple of houses, and Killinaboy Church off to your right up a side road, which is also worth a detour. A further 3.5km will bring you to Leamaneh Castle. Go right here on the R480 towards Ballyvaghan which will take you past Leamaneh Castle on your left. After 8km you will come to Poulnabrone Dolmen on your right, which is always worth a visit any time you pass it. Continue along the road for another 5km until you come to a sign for Aillwee Cave. Go right here and after 500m go right again into the Aillwee cave carpark.

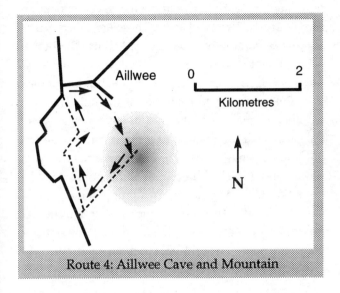

Route 4: Aillwee Cave and Mountain

Aillwee Cave is one of the main tourist attractions of County Clare. The entrance is sensitively built into the landscape, and inside is a coffee shop and souvenir shop to use while you wait for the next tour. The tour will give you all the basics about the cave system, including the bear pits at the entrance, the permanent temperature, the stalactites and how the system was discovered.

After you leave the cave, walk around the entrance uphill until you come to a drystone wall. Follow this up over the limestone pavement, with its clints and grikes, and you are walking directly above the cave. As limestone is a jointed rock, soluble in rainwater, the gaps between the individual blocks are progressively dissolved away. These are called grikes, and the remaining blocks are called clints. The Burren is famous for having many unusual Alpine and Arctic flowers and they are lovely to admire, but not to pick.

Follow the wall to the top of the hill. The view west across the rest of the Burren is very fine. At the top of the hill the wall takes a sharp turn to the left, but you continue across the 200m pavement to your right. You will be heading south at this point. It is a little similar to walking across an alpine glacier, with the need to avoid crevasses and pick the best route. All this will bring you to a track, and you go down this to the main road. Go right on the main road and back towards the Aillwee Cave and your car.

ROUTE 5
LEAMANEH CASTLE AND KILFENORA

Map: OS Discovery Series Map No. 51
Distance: 18km
Grade: Moderate
Average time: 5-6 hrs
Getting there from Ennis: Take the N85, which branches off the N18 at the roundabout at the northern end of Ennis. After approximately 4km go right on to the R476 at Fountain Crossroads. This road will bring you to Corrofin after another 9km approximately. Go along the main street of the town towards Kilfenora, and past the Garda station on the left at the far end of town. Approximately 1km past the Garda station is Inchiquin Lough, which is worth a short detour down a short track on the left. 3.5km beyond Corrofin you will come to Killinaboy village with a couple of houses, and Killinaboy Church off to your right up the side road, which is also worth a detour. A further 3.5km will bring you to Leamaneh Castle.
Parking: Park somewhere near the Castle.
Starting point: Irish National Grid reference M235935

Leamaneh Castle is one of the finest buildings of its sort in the west of Ireland. Originally built as a fifteenth-century tower house, it was extended in the early part of the seventeenth century as one of the main homes of the O'Briens who ruled this part of

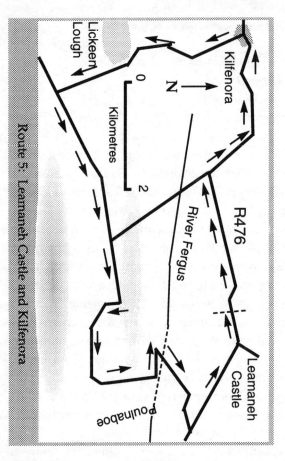

Route 5: Leamaneh Castle and Kilfenora

Lickeen Lough

Kilfenora

Kilometres

0

2

N

River Fergus

R476

Leamaneh Castle

Poulnaboe

west Munster since the time of Brian Boru in 1066. The contrast in building styles is not particularly evident from the road, but you will note the narrow windows at the southern end and the wide spacious ones in the

28

main house. The tower house also has a fire hole over the main entrance, which requires a big step as you climb the narrow spiral staircase. This was used to pour oil or arrows down on attackers in the event of them actually making it inside the house. The remains of the outer defences, called the bailey, are on the eastern side of the road. The narrow stairs also meant that attackers could only fight one to one with the defenders in any attack.

The main legend attached to the house is of the defenestration of a Cromwellian officer who had married the widow of the house. Maire Rua O'Brien's husband had been killed at the battle of Aughrim, and to retain the castle she married the new owner. It later transpired that he had been at Aughrim and compounded his error by insulting her husband. In revenge she threw him out of the topmost window of the Elizabethan mansion. Sadly, the landowner has barred access to the monument due to insurance worries, so you may not be able to stand at the top and look out over the extensive view, unless you are able to obtain permission.

Continue the walk by heading west from Leamaneh Castle towards Kilfenora on the R476. After 500m there is a track to your right which heads uphill to the north. Directly opposite this is a track leading into a farmyard. In the field south of this is Poulnacloneen Turlough which is the first feature unique to limestone geology on this walk. A turlough

29

can most simply be described as a fluctuating lake. In winter when the water table rises the level of the lake rises also. In summer the lake can dry out totally leaving cattle grazing in the empty space. There is no outflow visible on the surface as all the water flows underground. After Poulnacloneen you continue west towards Kilfenora in pleasant country.

You will reach Kilfenora after 4.5km, and there are two places of special interest. The first is the Burren Display Centre which gives a good overview of the geomorphology, archaeology and heritage of the area. The second is across the road in Kilfenora Cathedral with its series of High Crosses in the graveyard. After visiting the crosses take the road south from the middle of the village, which brings you very quickly out into the countryside again. Continue along the boreen passing various tracks and boreens. After 2.5km you come to your first intersection of four roads. Continue straight ahead heading south and around a sharp bend. Just beyond this sharp left is a little lake on your right hand side. 200m beyond this is a junction to your right. This leads to Lickeen Lough which is a pleasant place to take a break.

Return to the road and go right, south again. Heading south, you come to a sharp bend to your right followed after 100m by a sharp bend to your left. Continue along the road over the stream and at the next junction go left past the stand of conifers. Walk east for 3.5km until you come to a T-junction at

R227915. Go right here, and heading south go left at the next junction, Knockeighra, taking you east yet again. Continue east for another 1km before going left uphill to the north and Cahermacon.

The ground levels off, and 1km from the last junction you will be passing over one of the more interesting features of the area. Less than 300m on your right in the fields is Poulnaboe (the hollow of life) from which issues forth the River Fergus, the main river of south Clare. This is not the source of the river yet this is what happens. 600m to the west of the track you are on, the Fergus flows underground for a while to flow under the low hill you are standing on. The remains of the old Fergus Valley before it was captured by the underground stream is clearly visible above ground. It flows through one of the many cave systems in the area, before re-emerging at Poulnaboe. You should have no bother crossing the fields to the outfall, but this is private property. Explaining what you are doing, and why, works wonders in most situations, while demanding Rights of Way that do not exist usually gets the farmers back up. After Poulnaboe, go back to the road and go right. Head north past the houses on your left and right. At the next junction go right, which will take you east around a sharp bend after about 500m. Beyond this on your right is a megalithic tomb, just before a house. Once you reach the main road, R476, go left back to Leamaneh Castle and your car.

ROUTE 6

Map: OS Discovery Series Map No. 51

Distance: Route A – 10.5km

Route B – 20.5km

Grade: Moderate

Average time: Route A 3-4hrs

Route B 5-6hrs

Getting there from Ennis: Take the N85 which branches off the N18 at the roundabout at the northern end of Ennis. Follow this road until you reach Ennistimon after 24km and continue up the hill past the Protestant church on your left at the northern end of the town. Continue along to Lisdoonvarna 10km away until you come to Murphy's Bridge which is the second junction after you cross the Aille River. Go left here on to the R477 heading to Fanore until you descend through a series of sharp bends. On your right you will see the well-preserved Ballynalackan Castle.

Parking: Park anywhere near the Castle.

Starting point: Irish National Grid reference M101004

Two routes of varying difficulty begin at Ballynalackan Castle.

Route A: If you face towards the sea you are facing west. To the north, just beyond the entrance to Ballynalackan Castle and house, the start is on your right-hand side. It is marked by a little walking-man

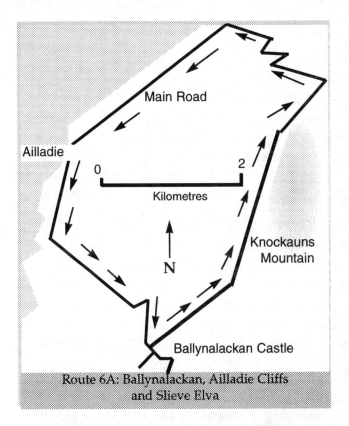

Main Road

Ailladie

0   2

Kilometres

N

Knockauns
Mountain

Ballynalackan Castle

Route 6A: Ballynalackan, Ailladie Cliffs
and Slieve Elva

sign as this is one of the major sections of the Burren
Way. Follow this road uphill heading towards Slieve
Elva, the highest point in the Burren. As you walk past
Knockauns Mountain you touch on the Clare shale
which overlays the limestone pavement. The
entrances to the known caves in this part of the
Burren can by found along this edge as the streams

33

which drain Slieve Elva reach the limestone and promptly disappear underground. The sinkholes which usually signify the entrance to the caves are in the fields to your left. On the surface you are passing through some of the most extensive pavement in the Burren so there are many unusual flowers and geological features in the fields.

After 4km the Burren Way, which is little more than a track at this stage, comes to a junction at M129049. Go left downhill and enjoy fine views of the Aran Islands to the west and northwest. Once you reach the main road R477 at a T-junction by a couple of houses, go left along the coast road south towards Ailladie. When you get to Ailladie you will come to a few lay-bys under a series of small cliffs. There may also be people camping in the fields on your right. If you go down the hill towards the coast you will come to the top of the Burren sea cliffs. These are some of the main and finest rock climbs in Ireland. Spare a thought for John Hawkins from Cork, one of Ireland's finest young climbers who died in a climbing accident in the French Alps in September 1998. He requested that his ashes be scattered over the Burren cliffs.

Once you are finished at Ailladie continue south along the coast road with the sea on your right for another 1km. Then the road takes a sharp left inland back to your starting point about 2km away.

Route B: Follow Route A as far as the left-hand junction descending to the coast at M129049.

Instead of descending continue to the next junction on the right by an old house at Balliny South. If you go right here (essentially around the house), you can go up to the summit of Slieve Elva. Walk up the track until you come to the next junction to the right after about 500m. Do not go right but continue straight up the mountain through the trees. At the top you reach the summit plateau and come to a T-junction where you go left. Follow the track westwards until it takes a sharp right turn and go north for about 200m. The summit is off to your left. Return the way you came back down to the house and go right with the sea now on your left-hand side downhill.

If you go straight on here you will come to the entrance to Faunarooska Cave, one of the more spectacular caves in the region. It is a sinkhole first mapped by a University of Bristol group in the 1960s who also discovered Doolin Cave, Poulgorm Cave and Glencurran Cave among others. It is 1,668m/ 5,743ft long and weaves down to Fanore Beg. It is unusual in that it is quite a steep cave while many of the others are practically level. It is no place for amateurs. The average temperature of the water in the cave is 13°C which makes it quite pleasant to wade through.

At the Y-junction at Faunarooska leave the Burren Way to go downhill. The walking-man sign points towards the Burren Way and the entrance to the

Faunarooska Cave but you take the right fork. This will lead you gently down to Fanore Beg and the coast. Once you reach the T-junction on the coast road R477 go left heading south towards Craggagh, which has a couple of pubs to take a break in. Continue south along the main road before swinging around the headland at Poulsallagh and back to your car at Ballynalackan.

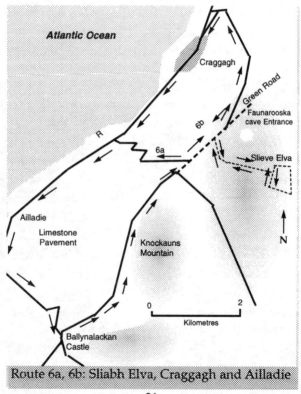

Route 6a, 6b: Sliabh Elva, Craggagh and Ailladie

ROUTE 7

THE GREEN ROAD ABOVE FANORE

Map: OS Discovery Series Map No. 51
Distance: 12km
Grade: Moderate
Average time: 4-5hrs
Getting there from Ennis: Follow directions to Lisdoonvarna from Route 6. From there, continue on to Murphy's Bridge which is the second junction after you cross the Aille River. Go right here on to the R477 heading to Fanore until you descend through a series of sharp bends. At the bottom of the bends you are joined by the R479 coming in from your left. Continue towards Fanore Bridge for about 10km.
Parking: Park once you reach Fanore Bridge. The church carpark is usually empty.
Starting point: Irish National Grid reference M146089

Take the third-class road east past the church on your right. You are walking up the Caher River valley with Gleninagh Mountain to your left and Slieve Elva to the right. This is classic Burren country with stubby trees, poor grass, pockets of shale and patches of naked limestone. After 1km the route departs from the Caher River and to your right is a set of impressive-looking cliffs. Continue along the route, which crosses the stream again and up the gently rising valley with the stream now on your right. The stream and the

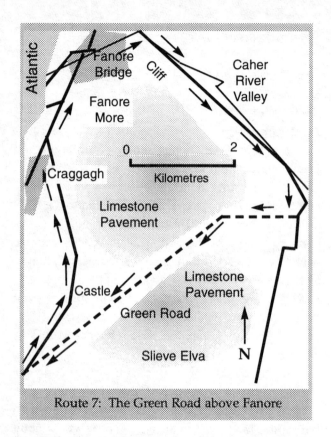

Route 7: The Green Road above Fanore

road join again at the next set of houses with a junction to your left. Continue straight to the next junction near a holy well. You have travelled approximately 3.5km. You are now joining the Burren Way and there should be a little walking-man sign to direct you right. Head 200m south to a track to your right at a ruined house. As this is on the Burren Way there should be another walking-man sign to direct you again at the start of the track. You are now on the famous Green Road above Fanore, which cuts straight across the limestone pavement.

Magnificent drystone walls bound it on either side as it passes through a part of Clare densely inhabited before the Great Famine, which wiped out whole communities in this area. The desolation of the landscape is immense with hardly even a windswept bush to keep you company. The track heads broadly west uphill, before turning southwest and out on to the open summit plateau of Slieve Elva. Continue along the Green Road over the plateau. You pass the ruins of Faunarooska Castle below you on the right, which was the seat of the McFeilims, one of the minor houses of the Dal Cais ruled by the O'Brien's. Less than 1km beyond the castle is a sharp turn to your right which brings you back below the castle. At this junction you leave the Burren Way and go right down to Fanore Beg 3km away. Once you reach the T-junction, right along the old road northwards towards Fanore More. This comes out at the school, and you are now on the main road, R477, 1km south of your start point. If you take the next left, this will bring you to Fanore strand, which is a pleasant way to end the day. Otherwise continue north to Fanore Bridge.

ROUTE 8
CORCOMROE ABBEY AND ABBEY HILL

Map: OS Discovery Series Map No. 51
Distance: 7.5km
Grade: Moderate
Average time: 2.5-3.5 hrs
Getting there from Galway: Leave Galway and head south at Oranmore towards Limerick on the N18. Pass through Clarinbridge, famous for its Oyster Festival, after 16km. At Kilcolgan, 18km from Galway, you branch right off the N18 at the end of the village near the petrol stations, which you come upon suddenly so be careful not to miss the turning. You are now on the N67 heading to Kinvarra, which is also a great spot to visit in its own right. Kinvarra is reached after 9km and continue along the Ballyvaghan Road. 12km from Kinvarra you reach Bell Harbour (Bealaclugga).
Parking: Park somewhere convenient to Bell Harbour.
Starting point: Irish National Grid reference M283083

This walk is moderately difficult and brings you out onto the open hill. Take the third-class road at the southern end of the village that leads east towards Corcomroe Abbey. The ground here is very flat as you are right down in the harbour. Continue up past the site of Corcomroe battlefield, where a battle was fought in 1317 as part of a minor civil war between two O'Brien factions for overall control of Thomond.

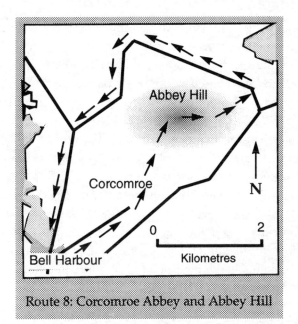

Route 8: Corcomroe Abbey and Abbey Hill

A short track leads left on to the battlefield and on your right are defensive earthworks associated with it. Return to the road and continue uphill towards Corcomroe Abbey, built between 1205 and 1225. This was one of the main Cistercian Abbeys in Ireland and there is hardly a more desolate spot on the island on which to build. If you look carefully you will notice that half the Abbey is made from dressed stone with fine ornamentation, while the other half is clearly far less pleasing to the eye. A famine in this part of Clare associated with the various disorders of the time meant that the Cistercians hadn't enough money to

41

pay for the completion of the Abbey. Still, the setting is dramatic and worth a visit on it own.

Continue north up the hill from the Abbey, which soon gives way to bare limestone pavement. This is a pest to walk over as you hop from grike to grike avoiding the gaps in between. It is slow going, but not too difficult if you take your time. The ground levels off as you near the summit and becomes very pleasant as you stroll to the summit cairn.

From the top of the hill you will be treated to one of the finest views of Galway, Galway Bay, Connemara and the Burren for comparatively little effort in hillwalking terms. Of course, if you are not used to hillwalking it is a bit of an effort, but worth it all the same.

To descend Abbey Hill keep Galway city and Galway Bay to your left, and walk downhill east-wards towards the track that circumnavigates the hill. Once you reach the track go left past the Holy Well after about 200m. Continue along for 1.5km from here to where the track takes a sharp left followed by another sharp left after 100m. It descends at a gentle angle for the next 700m before taking a sharp turn to the right almost at the bottom of the hill. This brings you to the main N67 after 1km and once you reach this, having kept left at the Y-junction, go back to Bell Harbour. This section of the walk is usually not pleas-ant on Bank Holiday weekends as the road becomes clogged with traffic.

ROUTE 9
TURLOUGH HILL AND SLIEVECARRAN

Maps: OS Discovery Series Maps No. 51 and 52
Distance: 15km
Grade: Difficult
Average time: 4-5 hrs
Getting there from Galway: Leave Galway and head south at Oranmore towards Limerick on the N18. Pass through Clarinbridge after 16km. At Kilcolgan, 18km from Galway, you branch right off the N18 at the end of the village near the petrol stations, which you come upon suddenly so be careful not to miss the turning. You are now on the N67 heading to Kinvarra, which is also a great spot to visit in its own right. Kinvarra is reached after 9km and continue along the Ballyvaghan road until after 7km you reach the County Clare border. On your left is Slievecallan. Once you cross the Clare border take the next turn on your left, and go sharp right around a tight bend. Continue down this road for 2km.
Parking: Park in the tiny village of Shanvally.
Starting point: Irish National Grid reference M297086.

The view to the east is of green fields, a few wind-blown trees and bare limestone. Behind your back the ruins of Corcomroe Abbey dominate the landscape. Looking east is one of those massive stone walls for which the Burren is famous. Slievecarran offers one of

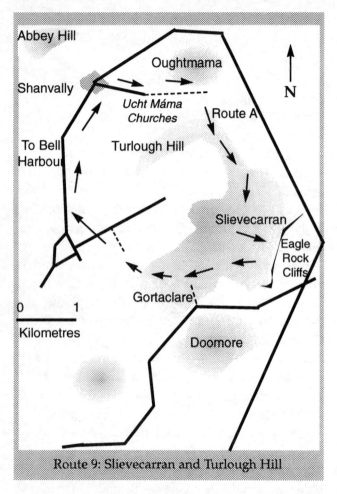

Abbey Hill

Oughtmama

Shanvally

N

Ucht Máma Churches

Route A

To Bell Harbour

Turlough Hill

Slievecarran

Eagle Rock Cliffs

0   1
Kilometres

Gortaclare

Doomore

Route 9: Slievecarran and Turlough Hill

the finest views over Galway Bay and Kinvarra Harbour. Kinvarra was one of the headquarters of Grace O'Malley, otherwise known as Granuaile, and

44

she controlled her pirate navy from Dungory Towerhouse perched on the edge of the sea, which can be seen from the top of these hills with ease.

From Shanvally go up the track east towards the Ucht Máma Churches and exit out onto the open hillside. Climb up to your left on to Oughtmama Slieve away from the churches and from the summit go south. You are now following a wall along the county boundary. Follow the wall downhill to the col, and then up gently towards the summit of the next hill. A drystone wall crosses your path on the Clare side. Follow this up to the summit of the hill at 251m. This was an Iron Age hillfort, and even in its ruined state is still terribly impressive given the fact that it's 4,000 years old. Return to the county boundary and go right, heading south, still following the wall. Go downhill to the col where another wall comes in from your right. Continue along uphill until the wall takes a sharp left downhill, and go right here uphill to the summit of Slievecarran, which is hidden behind yet another stone wall. From the summit cairn go south until another wall bars your path. Cross this and go right westwards.

Alternatively, follow it east for 100m, then south for 400m, and then sharp left for 200m. You will come suddenly to the top of Kinallia, and a superb view east. Be extremely careful here when you approach the edge as the cliff in front of you is 150m or 500 ft high. At the edge you will be looking straight down on Saint Colman's Oratory and the Eagles Rock bird sanctuary. Follow the wall back to the summit plateau.

Continue along west towards Gortaclare Mountain over yet another wall that comes in from your left and past an old rath also on your left. The wall goes sharp right here, but stick to the ridge leaving the wall behind. This takes you southwest, until you reach yet another wall blocking your path after 350m. Go right here, and when the wall goes sharp left, follow it to the summit at 295m. It then goes right downhill and follow it down to the road. This being limestone country, your way may be barred by some small cliffs, but you can avoid all difficulties by going either left or right.

At the bottom of the hill, go left along the road. Continue westwards, down the road to a T-junction and go right. At the next junction keep right and heading north you come to the village of Turlough. It is 4km north along the road back to your car in Shanvalley. After 2.5km a junction leads left into Bealaclugga (Bell Harbour), but continue straight on to Shanvally.

ROUTE 10
MULLAGH MORE

Maps: OS Discovery Series Maps No. 51 and 52
Distance: 14.5km
Grade: Moderate
Average time: 3.5-4.5 hrs
Getting there from Galway: Leave Galway and head south at Oranmore on the N18 towards Limerick until you reach Gort. Go right in the centre of Gort and follow the R460. This road takes a right after about 300m at a crossroads in the town. Continue along this road for 9km approximately until you come to Lough Bunny on your right. 2km after Lough Bunny you come to Ballyeighter Woods on your left.
Parking: Park anywhere near Ballyeighter Woods.
Starting point: Irish National Grid reference M345942

Mullagh More is the essential Burren, but it is an extremely fragile landscape so this walk does not go onto open mountain. A Visitor Centre is being built on the southside of the mountain amid some controversy. A track leads south into Ballyeighter Woods and directly opposite this is a third-class road leading northwards. Walk up this road with Mullagh More on your left. This is the classic Burren vista with the bare limestone, rough trees and branches so common to these uplands. Continue up the road on flat pavement

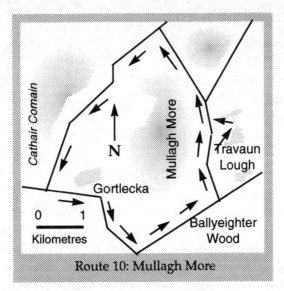

Route 10: Mullagh More

with Mullagh More's steep eastern face dominating the view. As you pass gently rising ground on your right you should make a slight detour to Travaun Lough, the largest of four interconnected lakes. Not surprisingly the whole area is riddled with caves, and the outflow of the whole system is under Travaun Lough. At the next Y-junction go left and the ground gently rises as you come around the northern end of Mullagh More. 1.5km from the junction you come to a T-junction and you go left. Follow this around a bend to the right, and after a further 100m go left to Knockans Lower. The high ground of Mullagh More will be due south of you now. Continue southwest down this road and after 1.5km, change to the right hand side of Discovery map 51 where the white is, and count the numbers up to 97. The next minor road above this is the one you are on. Continue south through the heart of the National Park until you come to a crossroads about 3km from where the map changes. This will take you past Glenquin church on your left which is worth a look. At the next crossroads go left eastwards and down past Gortalecka on your left, before the road takes a sharp right. Continue along for 600m and you join map 52 again at R320934. Continue and go left once you reach the T-junction with the R460. It is about 3km back to your car but the views over the Cullaun River system are very pleasant.

Route 11
Poulnabrone Dolmen and the Castletown River

Map: OS Discovery Series Map No. 51
Distance: 13.5km
Grade: Moderate
Average time: 4.5-5 hrs
Getting there from Ennis: Follow Route 4 to Poulnabrone Dolmen.
Starting point: Irish National Grid reference M235004.

Poulnabrone Dolmen appears on everything to do with Ireland, along with Guinness, round towers, shamrocks, Slea Head and the Four Courts. Just inside the fence on your right is a perfect amphitheatre in the limestone. This is probably caused by a collapsed cave system underneath, but unless it is investigated it is hard to tell.

Continue across the limestone pavement to reach the tomb in a couple of minutes. In its present state there are a few large upright stones capped by a large flat capstone. Carbon dating of the soil underneath the megalith suggests that the tomb was built 3,000 years ago. This means that people were busily constructing these 2,500 years before Columbus discovered America. It originally looked like a mound of stones, but these have been stripped away over the millennia. Off to the left people have taken to building their own mini-dolmens in a sort of unofficial sculpture park.

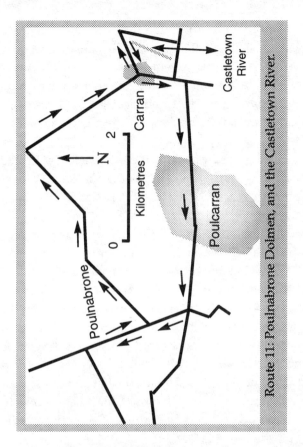

Route 11: Poulnabrone Dolmen, and the Castletown River.

Just beyond the dolmen to the east is one of the dry canyons that are so common in the Burren. The stream that flowed down here has long since been captured upstream by a swallow hole and disappeared underground. The dolmen looks particularly well from this angle.

Once you return to the road turn left and at the next junction go left eastwards. This minor road takes you out across the pavement with unusual views of the dry valley and Poulnabrone to your left. Near Poulaphuca turn right and descend onto the main road to Carran 3km away. This is a good spot for a break.

Continue east towards the UCG Field Centre and just beyond this on the right the Castletown River appears overground for a short period before going underground all the way to the Fergus.

Return the way you came back into Carran and go left south before taking the next right which will take you downhill into the heart of Poulcarran. This is one of the large turloughs that make up so much of the landscape of this part of Clare and walking along the road, you get a very good idea of how a turlough operates with the drainage at the bottom of the feature and high ground on all sides. Pass under the main ESB line up the hill and after 1km you come to a cross-roads at the main road. Go right north here and walk up the side of the main road for 2km back towards Poulnabrone.

Route 12
FINVARRA POINT AND BALLYVAGHAN BAY

Maps: Os Discovery Series Map No. 51
Distance: 9km
Grade: Easy
Average time: 2.5-3.5 hrs
Getting there from Galway: Follow the directions to Kinvarra from Route 8. Continue along the road between Kinvarra and Bell Harbour for 10km until you reach Ballyvelaghan Lough on your right. Take the turn to the right at the western end of the lough, just as the main road takes a sharp left towards Bell Harbour.
Parking: Park here at the western end of Ballyvelaghan Lough.
Starting point: Irish National Grid reference M277113

This walk moves away from the inland Burren and has the added attraction of being short. Once you have parked your car go to the western end of Ballyvelaghan Lough, and go northwest up the third-class road off the main N67 between Bell Harbour and Kinvara. Pass a junction to your right, and continuearound the sharp turn to your left. The road is wonderfully straight at this point. After 500m the sea appears on your left with lovely views into Bell Harbour and across to Muckinish Point. Continue along the road which takes you back inland to

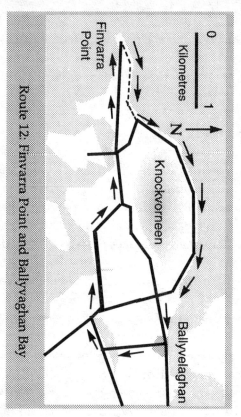

Finvarra and go sharp left. Head west past the village and continue along the minor road until you meet the sea again on your left. A causeway will bring you on a detour out to Scanlans Island if you wish, which is worth it only if you have time to spare.

From the junction to Scanlans Island continue west. If you are feeling tired take the next junction to your right and 3km off the walk. Alternatively, continue west towards Finavarra Point and its ruined Martello tower 1.5km west of the junction. This gives wonderful views of Ballyvaghan Bay and west towards Slieve Elva and Black Head. Continue along the track around the northern side of the narrow headland which brings you back to the public road at Lough Murree. Pass Lough Murree on your right and walk along the coast around Knockvorneen Hill. Continue east after the next junction to the post office at New Quay and take the next right at the pier. Go down this road heading south and cross Ballyvelaghan Lough by the causeway back on to the main road. Go right and head west back to your car.

ROUTE 13
COOLE PARK, GORT, CO. GALWAY

Map: OS Discovery Series Map No. 52
Distance: 2km
Grade: Easy
Average time: 30 minuntes plus Visitor Centre
Getting there from Galway: Leave Galway and head south on the N18 towards Limerick. After 33km, having passed through Oranmore, Kilcolgan and Ardrahan you will come to Coole Park Visitor Centre. Many road signs will direct you to the right but if you reach Gort you've missed it. Drive into the demesne.
Parking: Park in the well laid out carpark.
Starting point: Irish National Grid reference: M441050
Coole Park was the home of Lady Augusta Gregory, one of the leading lights in the Celtic Revival, which included W.B. Yeats, one of Ireland's most famous writers. Indeed one of his most famous poems 'The Wild Swans at Coole' was written here. The big house did not survive the War of Independence and was pulled down in the 1940s despite a huge campaign to save it so the visitor centre is housed in the stables. However, it is a very fine show and worth the money. After the centre it is time for a walk in the grounds.

The walk will take you around in a circle and down to the lake. Here Yeats gained inspiration for many of his most famous poems and in the pristine

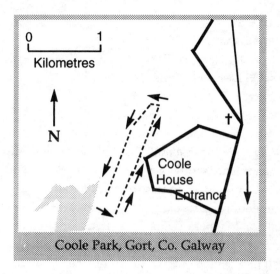

parkland it is difficult not to be inspired. Continue through the trees back to the house and a well-deserved break in the coffee shop. Over the main road less than 1km away is Thoor Ballylee Tower House in which Yeats lived out his later years and this is also worth a visit. However, walking there is not advisable as this would involve crossing a particularly fast stretch of the N18 twice.

ROUTE 14
LOUGH GRANEY

Map: OS Discovery Series Map No. 52

Distance: 18.5km

Grade: Difficult

Average time: 5-6 hrs

Getting there from Galway: Take the N18 from Galway to Gort. 5km south of Gort take the Scarriff Road R461. Continue along this road through the village of Drumandoora after 6km. The road rises over the north flank of Maghera, with its RTE transmitter on the summit, and then downhill with Lough Graney straight ahead. Continue down off the col under the steep eastern slopes of Maghera along the R461. You pass a broadleaf forest on your right just before you come to a T-junction. The R461 to the right leads to Scarriff, the road to the left leads to Caher and Lough Graney. Continue along the road into Caher.

Parking: Park here. If you did nothing more than sit here and admire the lake it is worth it.

Starting point: Irish National Grid reference R564907

This is a pleasant walk with an optional bit of ascent for the view west towards the Burren. Right on the edge of the large conifer forest that has shrouded East Clare and West Galway, the walk gives you a good idea of how extensive this commercial forest is. Head east past the Post Office in the small village of Caher

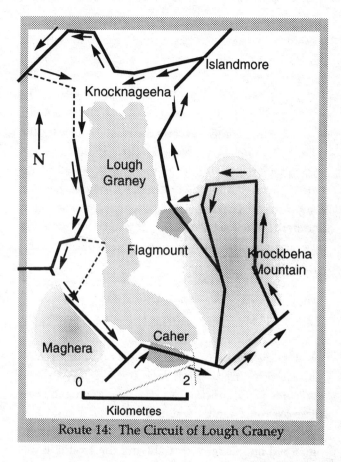

Route 14: The Circuit of Lough Graney

The lake's name translates as 'the lake of the sun'. Walk along the shore and cross the bridge over the Caher River. A large stone stands here, which is the spot where Brian Merriman is reputed to have written *The Midnight Court*. Possibly the most famous poem in the Irish language, it is an attack on the standards of society at the time. Continue along the road with old oak and birch woods to your left past the old national school on your left.

The hump of Knockbeha mountain now lies to the northeast. This is the main objective for the day but is also optional. Continue along the road away from the lake as the trees begin to peter out on your left. You come to a junction 2km from the start leading to your left. This is just after the old national school. There is a signpost for Feakle pointing the way you came and another for the East Clare Way. If you go left you will be going broadly north and you will avoid the climb up Knockbeha, and miss the views from the top.

To climb Knockbeha go straight on at this junction to the next one, about 200m away. A track leads left up the hill which is steep enough but not as steep as the ground to your left. You climb 80m over 1km so it is tough going. The ground then levels off quite dramatically and the track bends left after about 300m and you come to a Y-junction. You are now joining the East Clare Way and a little walking-man sign should give you some comfort. Take the left fork uphill past a couple of old houses on your right and the ground levels off. If you wish you can go left here and head west onto the summit at 295m, a distance of 350m, for a lovely view over the lake. With the lake at your back and the conifers on your left-hand side, return the way you came back to the track. You are heading east.

Once you return to the track go left heading north downhill past the conifers. The track takes a sharp left after 300m and wends its way gradually down the hill. You join the tarred road at a T-junction and go left. After 250m the East Clare Way takes a right directly the village of Flagmount.

Once you reach the village you have a choice: (1) Go left and head southwards past the church back towards your car. After 2km you come to the T-junction where you turn right taking you along beside the lake back to your car; (2) Turn right at the church and head north with the lake to your left, all of which is on the East Clare Way. Continue along this, passing Caher wood and bird sanctuary on your right after 1.5km. The road swings to your left just beyond the wood and then swings right after 400m. Shortly a track on your left leads into a set of picnic tables overlooking the lake. This is a good place to take a break for lunch, but beware of the midge swarms in the summer months.

After your visit to the picnic tables return to the road the way you came. Once on the road continue north through the trees to the bridge over the Bleach River. Follow the East Clare Way signs left around the sharp bend. The road takes a sharp right after 200m but the East Clare Way goes straight on west with the river on your left-hand side. Continue along this track through the woods. You will come to a T-junction after 2km and go left along the road to Derrycarran.

Continue along the road for 1.5km.

You have to get this next section of the walk right so take special care to follow the little walking-man signs. Once you enter the trees the East Clare Way passes between two low hills which may not be terribly clear. After 500m it swings gently right and then left. Shortly after the left the East Clare Way goes down a track with a sign. Continue along this track until you come to a junction and go left and then right almost immediately. The track swings right after approximately 400m and 1km from here the track takes a sharp left at Spaightspark. After 500m you come to a lovely vista across the lake to Flagmount. Continue along the trail uphill away from the lake and cross the shoulder of the hill ahead at Doorus West. From here you get a fine view of Maghera. At the top of the hill go southwards, downhill to the R461. Follow the R461 past the old broadleaf stand on your right to a T-junction. Go left here back into Caher and your car.

ROUTE 15
CLARE LAKELANDS AND CRAGGAUNOWEN

Maps: OS Discovery Series Map No. 58
Distance: 11km
Grade: Moderate
Average time: 3-4 hrs
Getting there from Limerick: Leave Limerick on the N18 to Galway and after 4km take the Sixmilebridge road R462 through Cratloe. You reach Sixmilebridge 7km after turning off the main Ennis road. Continue up the main street with the river on your left to Kilmurry. Go through Kilmurry towards Quin on the R462. At the Y-junction 1km to the north of the village go left. 2km beyond this you reach Sadlier's Cross Roads. *Parking*: Park carefully at the Sadlier's Cross Roads.
Starting point: Irish National Grid reference R463718

This is a short walk all on roads and tracks in the heart of the lake district in South Clare. The undoubted star of the show is Craggaunowen, which, unlike Samuel Johnson's description of the Giants Causeway, is worth seeing and worth going to see. From Sadlier's Cross Roads take the road northwards which is signposted for Craggaunowen. Walk along this with a fine view of the lakes from a low hill after 1km. On your left from this vantage point you will get your first view of Craggaunowen Castle and Heritage Centre. Descend along the road northwards and up again until you

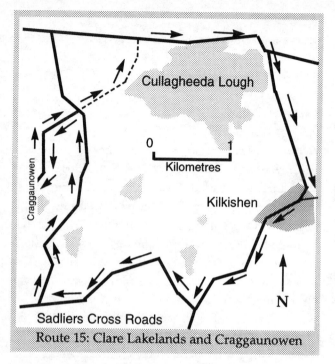

Cullagheeda Lough

0   1
Kilometres

Craggaunowen

Kilkishen

N

Sadliers Cross Roads

Route 15: Clare Lakelands and Craggaunowen

come to a sign for Craggaunowen. You will soon reach the castle, which is in fact a 15th-century tower house similar to many of the others in this part of Clare. However, the main attraction is the *crannóg* or lake village built in the lake beside the castle.

Crannógs were one of the most defensible of native Irish dwellings and especially popular in this part of Clare. This reconstruction is well done and should not be missed. However, you do have to pay, so be aware of this.

Continue west past the castle and you will pass a megalith on your right as the road swings left sharply. Continue along through the trees and at the next junction go right northwards, and then east back onto the main north/south road. Here you join another section of the East Clare Way. Continue along the track directly opposite you through the wood. This is very pleasant and you get good views of Lough Cullaunyheeda to your right through the trees. Practically at the other end of the woods the track bends left and comes to a T-junction. Go right here and you are soon walking by the lake shore. After 1.2km you come to another T-junction. Turn right and head south towards Kilkishen on the R462. Take care here as this is the main road between Tulla and Sixmilebridge. After 2km you come to Kilkishen, a nice little spot to stop for a rest.

Continue on the Sixmilebridge road, R462, from Kilkishen past the castle on your right after a little over 1km. Then the road bends to your left. Beyond this is a tiny lake on your right called Loch an Chaisleán or Castle Lake and a road to your right. You go up this heading off the R462 northwest. This brings you once again by the lakes and has the added attraction of being quiet. After 700m the road turns left and a short while after this you pass Shandangan Lough on your left. The ground rises gently from here over the low ridge ahead, and as you pass under the main ESB line for Clare, you are almost home. Down to the junction 300m away and right back to your car.

ROUTE 16
CAHER MOUNTAIN, LOUGH DERG AND TUAMGRANEY

Maps: OS Discovery Series Map No. 58
Distance: 14km
Grade: Difficult
Average time: 4-5 hrs
Getting there from Limerick: Leave Limerick and head north on the R464 Killaloe road along the side of the Ardnacrusha headrace towards Parteen, reached after 2km. Cross the bridge here and go into Parteen. Pass the school and church on your right and go left at the next crossroads on the R463 to Parkroe. At the Y-junction in the middle of the village go right off the Broadford road onto the Killaloe road, R463. This involves a sharp right over the Blackwater, and out along the side of the headrace towards the huge weir at the top of the Headrace 10km away. 14km from Parkroe you reach Killaloe. Continue through Killaloe and out the R463 Scarriff Road, along the western bank of the Shannon. You are now driving by the side of Lough Derg, which is a very fine drive on its own. At Ogonnelloe, reached after 8km, the road bends around into Scarriff Bay, which is lovely countryside. *Parking* :1km after the village you come to a parking lay-by and park here.
Starting point: Irish National Grid reference R678823

This walk has lovely views of Lough Derg, and other

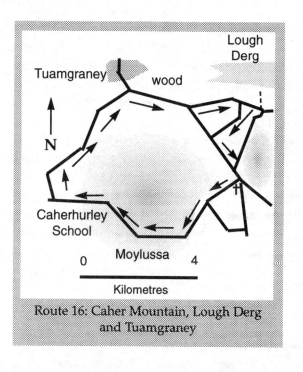

Route 16: Caher Mountain, Lough Derg and Tuamgraney

than a gentle bit of uphill to acquire the view, is not terribly taxing. Leave your car at the picnic tables and go west along the road to the next junction. A track leads downhill to the lake and a ruined castle. However, we are going left uphill on the sideroad which is gentle enough and zig-zags before rising after a sharp bend to the left uphill southwards to a col between two hills. Go left at the T-junction and head south through the col to the far end. At the junction of four roads by the church, you go right. Directly ahead of you to the south is the steep north slope of Moylussa, the highest hill in the Slieve Bearnagh and in County Clare. Off to your left is Lough Derg as it heads south to Killaloe so the view is quite fine, especially from below the churchyard, a little detour to the south.

From the crossroads the road rises gently, uphill, northwest and you join the East Clare Way at the next junction. Continue gently uphill onto the ridge past a small stand of conifers on your right and under the northern slopes of Moylussa. Continue along the track as it heads broadly westwards and then drops gently down until it takes a sharp bend to the left below Knocknalecka, 2km from where you crossed the ridge. Follow along past Caherhurly National School on your left. When you reach the next crossroads, about 300m beyond the school, go right downhill, northwards along the East Clare Way. It weaves its way beside a couple of conifer plantations and up over Malthouse Hill, before dropping down to the main R463 just to the south of Tuamgraney village. If you have time, go into Tuamgraney, which has a heritage centre and what is probably the oldest working church in Ireland. After this an optional walk in the wood is recommended, before you take the R463 east, 4km back to your car.

ROUTE 17

KILLALOE, FEENLEA MOUNTAIN AND LOUGH DERG

Map: OS Discovery Series Map No. 58
Distance: 11km
Grade: Difficult
Average time: 3.5-4.5 hrs
Getting there from Limerick: Leave Limerick and head north on the R464 Killaloe road along the side of the Ardnacrusha Headrace towards Parteen reached after 2km. Cross the bridge here and go left into Parteen. Pass the school and church on your right and go left at the next crossroads on the R463 to Parkroe. At the Y-junction in the middle of the village go right off the Broadford road on to the Killaloe road. Go sharp right over the Blackwater, and out along the side of the Headrace towards the huge weir at the top of the Headrace 10km away. 14km from Parkroe you reach Killaloe.
Parking: Park next to the Roman Catholic Church, at the top of the hill next to the Garda station.
Starting point: Irish National Grid reference R700729

Brian Boru was the first high king of Ireland to defeat the Norse invaders who controlled County Clare from their base in Limerick. Sadly, following the rebellion of the Dublin Norsemen, he was slain at the Battle of Clontarf in 1014. From the Dal Cais, Clare's main family in the 10th century, his great capital was at Kincora,

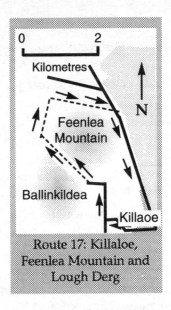

0   2
Kilometres

N

Feenlea
Mountain

Ballinkildea

Killaoe

Route 17: Killaloe,
Feenlea Mountain and
Lough Derg

around which the town of Killaloe grew and which was also one of the main crossing points of the Shannon south of Lough Derg. A visit to the heritage centre, which is open in the summer, is again recommended to give you a feel for the area. You should also visit Killaloe Cathedral which was built in the 12th century and is a very fine building. However, the star of the show is the Roman Catholic Church, with St Lua's Oratory rescued from the Shannon in 1929 before it was flooded by the Ardnacrusha hydro-electric scheme. Inside the church is a magnificent Harry Clarke stained-glass window, which is a must see for anyone visiting Killaloe.

From Killaloe take the East Clare Way west out of the town on the small road between the Garda station on your left and the church on your right. Continue out of the town past the garages on your right up the hill. In the fields on your left are a couple of standing stones which are worth a look. Once over the brow of the hill the road continues stright for a while. After 2km you come to a crossroads just after a laneway to your left and go right here. There is a layby to your left by the stream, which is a good place to stop.

Continue northwards away from the laybay towards Feenlea Mountain which is today's main objective. Pass a couple of houses on your left after 600m and 300m beyond these take a junction to your left uphill and westwards. This is on the East Clare Way so a little walking-man sign should help you along. After a further 300m the road takes a sharp right. Here the East Clare Way goes straight on and you follow along the side of a pleasant river valley with the stream far below you on the left. On the other side of the valley are the lower slopes of Moylussa. Continue uphill and then away from the stream to the col between Moylussa and Feenlea. Once you reach the edge of the forestry you have the option of going right along the ridge to Feenlea summit 700m away at 383m for a fine view over Lough Derg and the Shannon Basin.

Return to the forestry by going west along the ridge. This means that Lough Derg should be behind

your back. Once back on the track go right northwards through the trees. Take any of the tracks to your
right as they all join up. Continue along this track as it
leads eastwards around the mountain. After 1.5km it
doubles back on itself and 300m later it swings back
again to rejoin the route about 15m below the first
hairpin. Most people will take the shortcut as the
temptation is too great.

Continue down through the trees and another
couple of zig-zags to the road by the side of Lough
Derg just south of Rinnaman point. The picnic tables
at Rinnaman are a nice enough spot for lunch.

From here go south along the side of the lake, to
your left, towards Killaloe past the Craglea woods on
your right. From the end of the wood to Killaloe you
pass through ribbon development which is so hated
by environmental correspondents and so loved by
ordinary people. The housing disappears on your left
as you reach Kincora wood beside the Shannon.
Continue into the town and back to your car.

Route 18

O'Briensbridge and the Ardnacrusha Headrace Canal

Map: OS Discovery Series Map No. 58

Distance: 8km

Grade: Easy

Getting there from Limerick: Leave Limerick by the Dublin Road, and after 8km branch off this at Castleconnell for O'Briensbridge. Cross the bridge, over the Shannon and go left up the main street before crossing the bridge over the Headrace Canal. At the next crossroads go straight through towards Bridgetown on the R466.

Parking: Park once you drive through the junction.

Starting point: Irish National Grid reference R657670

This is a short walk with the added interest of visiting the start of the Headrace Canal that takes water 11km to Ireland's first major power station at Ardnacrusha. One of the largest civil engineering projects of its time, it was described in the Dáil as 'Paddy McGilligan's Mad Scheme', such was the breadth of vision that it incorporated. Building the power station in 1929 would have been a major achievement for a country which had just gained independence, but diverting the pent up energies of the River Shannon too in record time, under budget, and without fuss was an outstanding achievement rarely matched in subsequent

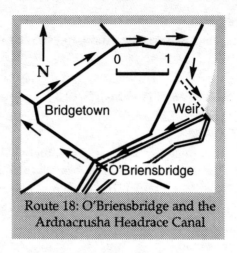

Route 18: O'Briensbridge and the
Ardnacrusha Headrace Canal

years by any Irish government.

After parking, walk westwards towards Bridgetown on the Broadford road. Continue along for 1.5km. Just before the church turn right northwards and pass the school on your right. After 100m at the T-junction, go right towards Killaloe. At the next junction stay on this road keeping right, as it brings you out into open countryside very quickly. After 1.5km you cross the Black River at Aughayatha. Continue into Ardbacartan Cross Roads and instead of going sharp left towards Killaloe veer right on past the houses down the hill. There is a sign for 'Sarsfields Ride 1690' pointing left uphill at this junction. Continue along going sharp left and then sharp right after 300m. A further 500m on this road leads to the Ardcloony River and follow this down to the main road about 150m away.

The main road is part of the Lough Derg Way and once you reach it cross carefully to the far side. Walk south down the road and take the next left which should be signed as part of the Lough Derg Way. Once you reach the river which is nearly 1km wide at this point, go right southwards towards the large weir where the Shannon divides. Follow the river bank along the side of the headrace canal with fine views across to O'Brienbridge. Once you reach the bridge 3km from where you joined the Shannon go right back to your car.

ROUTE 19
MOYLUSSA: THE HIGHEST MOUNTAIN IN CLARE

Map: OS Discovery Series Map No. 58
Distance: 13km
Grade: Difficult
Getting there from Limerick: Leave Limerick by the Dublin Road and after 8km branch off this at Castleconnell for O'Brienbridge. Just before O'Briensbridge you reach Montpelier. Cross the bridge, and go left up the main street before crossing the bridge over the Headrace Canal for Ardnacrusha. At the next cross roads go straight on across the Killaloe Road towards Bridgetown. Go through Bridgetown on the Broadford Road and after 5km you come to a very sharp left. You pass under the main ESB line and 2km from the sharp bend is a signpost to your right for the village of Kilbane. Turn right down this road. *Parking*: Park by the bridge in the middle of the village.
Starting point: Irish National Grid reference R620725

Along with Slievecarran in the Burren this is one of the more difficult walks in the book, and definitely not the one you start with if you are a beginner. From Kilbane follow the East Clare Way northwest past the school and take the second turning on the right after that. This is reached after about 1km from the village. The East Clare Way goes up here so there should be

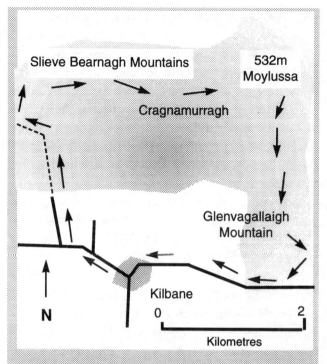

Slieve Bearnagh Mountains

532m
Moylussa

Cragnamurragh

Glenvagallaigh
Mountain

Kilbane

N

0   2

Kilometres

Route 19: Moylussa: the highest mountain in Clare

signs to help you. Continue up the road past the old church and graveyard on your right. Where the road turns left at a couple of houses, go straight on up the road following the East Clare Way. Where this track peters out the East Clare Way goes west, and you stay on it until you cross the stream. After you have crossed the stream go right uphill to the col between point marked 335m to your left and the steeper hill to your right. You shortly arrive on the wide boggy col.

Go right along the ridge uphill heading east on to the main ridge of the Slieve Bearnagh hills. If you stick to the ridge you will come to Lough Avillig just under the summit of the first hill. The ground rises a few metres and descends just a little before rising up to the summit of Cragnamurragh. There is a fine view in all directions except east which is dominated by Moylussa.

As you descend from the summit heading east you come to some of the unkempt wall that runs along the top of these hills. Once again this was built in the 18th century to delimit the extent of two estates. Follow the wall along to the lower slopes of Moylussa and wade across the bog and heather to the summit plateau. There are two high points, one at the southern and one at the northern end. Weave your way between the two streams, trying to stay dry, and once on the summit go right to the southern end of the plateau. The ground falls away very steeply in front of you into the Ardcloony valley, so it is best not to descend this way, unless you are a regular hillwalker, even though it looks very inviting. The best thing to do is to return west the way you came to Cragnamurragh and from the col just before the rise on to this (at 492m) go south along the ridge to Glenvagalliagh Mountain 1km to the south. Once you reach Glenvagalliagh Mountain continue south down the ridge until you come to the trees. Follow the line of the trees west until you come to a track leading south into the forest. Turn left onto this and follow it downhill and around the forest westwards. You come to a junction in the track with one leading left down-hill. Ignore this and continue straight on through the trees. This brings you down to the road and East Clare Way that goes over the col between Glenvagalliagh Mountain behind you and Lackareagh Mountain ahead of you. You have rejoined the East Clare Way and a little walking-man sign may direct you. Go right downhill out of the trees with very fine views into the valley ahead and back to Kilbane, visible ahead of you 2km away.

ROUTE 20
CRATLOE WOOD AND WOODCOCK HILL

Map: OS Discovery Series Map No. 58
Distance: Route A – 5km
        Route B – 10km
Grade: Route A – Moderate
     Route B – Moderate
Average time: Route A – 1.5-2.5 hrs
           Route B – 2.5-3.5 hrs
Getting there from Limerick: Leave Limerick on the N18
to Galway and after 4km take the Sixmilebridge road
R462 to Cratloe. Pass under the railway line and short-
ly after Cratloe crossroads turn right. At the end of the
built up area a sign for Cratloe woods takes you right
uphill to the wood 1km away.
Parking: Park in the woods by the side of Lough
Gorteen. Alternatively park in the village.
Starting point: Irish National Grid reference. R488623

Two Aircraft Navigation Beacons can be found on the
summit of Woodcock Hill which dominates the view
north from Limerick. This walk takes you through
Cratloe Wood and to the top of Woodcock Hill for a
fine view over Limerick. Cratloe Wood is a fine place
to visit on its own. However, when combined with
Woodcock Hill it becomes a fine walk with splendid
views out over the Shannon estuary and Limerick city.
Park at the picnic tables beside Lough Gorteen and

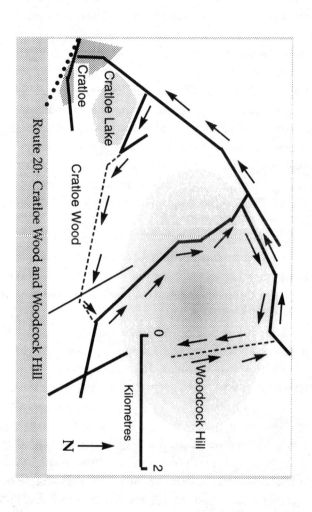

Route 20: Cratloe Wood and Woodcock Hill

Cratloe Lake

Cratloe

Cratloe Wood

Woodcock Hill

Kilometres

0

2

N →

81

follow the track up towards the viewing point above the lake. From the viewing point return eastwards toward the hairpin bend and here continue along the track-cum-firebreak that leads from the point of the bend. This is the main track through the woods and all others mentioned are minor, so it is quite clear which way to take. After 200m go left at a junction along the face of the hill and continue along this, crossing a well-hidden stream. The track bends right around the other side of the little valley and at the next Y-junction after 500m you take the left fork. This takes you across the hill for 300m until your path is crossed by another track just above a stream ahead. Continue across the stream and out of the woods on to a side road.

Go left on this uphill out of the trees, and past a farm on your right. Continue uphill back through trees and on to the ridge ahead at Gallows Hill. You are now 2.3km from where you turned left onto the road out of the woods. At the end of the trees just as the road starts to descend a road leads along the ridge to your right. If you have had enough take the next left down hill to your car 2km away in Cratloe Wood.

Option B: If you wish to continue the walk, take the road leading right along the ridge at Gallows Hill, mentioned above. Continue along this past another stand of conifers on your right until you come to the entrance to the Beacons about 2km from the right turn. Go south up this track towards the Beacons, but stay out of the compound as you are not welcome here. Go beyond the towers heading south for no more than 100m and enjoy the view of the river and the city. Return the way you came past the beacons back to the road. Go left down the road until it comes to the T-junction at Gallows Hill reached after 2km. Go right here and take the next left almost immediately. This takes you along the ridge south for 200m through Castlequarter and then down westwards for 500m before turning left and southwest downhill for 1.5km back to your car at Cratloe Woods.

ROUTE 21
DYSERT O'DEA

Map: OS Discovery Series Map No. 57
Distance: 6km
Grade: Easy
Average time: 1.5-2.5hrs
Getting there from Ennis: Leave Ennis by the N85, which branches off the N18 at the roundabout at the northern end of the town. After approximately 4km go right on to the R476 at Fountain Crossroads. This road will lead towards Corrofin. After 6km a large sign for the Dysert O'Dea Archaeology Centre brings you down a road to your left. A junction to your right brings you to the Archaeology Centre, which is situated in an old Tower house.
Parking: You can park on the road in the centre.
Starting point: Irish National Grid reference. R283850

Even if you only drove to Dysert O'Dea and visited the Church it would be a nice day out. A lovely walk, the history of Ireland from the fifth century through the Norman Conquest and beyond is written in the stones. The Archaeology Centre provides a full history of the various monuments including the castle, high cross and 6th-century church with its alleged sheila-na-gig over the entrance door. There is also a description of the Battle of Dysert O'Dea in 1318, where Felim O'Brien defeated a Norman army led by de Clare. This included

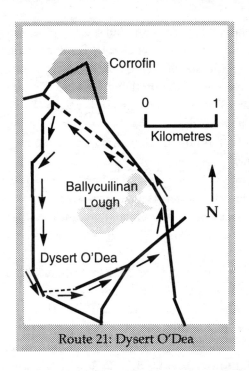

Route 21: Dysert O'Dea

the slaughter of 60 knights with de Clare amongst them. The virtual defeat of Felim's men in the face of superior forces was assured, only to be rescued by the arrival of the O'Deas and O'Briens in the nick of time. In all about 600 people took part in the battle. A marked circuit of the various monuments is provided.

After your visit to the centre, walk eastwards along the road to a junction and continue east towards the main Corrofin road R476. At the road go left northwards towards Corrofin. The battle of Dysert O'Dea took place in the fields on your left. The oak woods in which de Clare was butchered by Felim are long since gone. At the stream which flows into Ballycullinan Lough you leave the battlefield behind. Continue for another 500m until the lake abuts the road, and take the side road that leaves the main road going left. Sitting by the side of the lake is as good a spot as any for lunch.

Continue along the undulating track under the main ESB line after 1km. Pass a track on your left about 300m after the power line, and another road leading to the R476 on your right. Take the next road on the left just before you reach the Corrofin/ Milltown Malbay road at Beggars Bridge. Walk down the road back under the main ESB line and past Gahernamona Castle on your left after 1km.

Continue south along the road for 1km and you will see Dysert O'Dea church on your left. The church was built in AD738 by St Tola and is still used as a graveyard. At the eastern end of the site a stile leads to the fields to Dysert O'Dea High Cross which shows Christ crucified and Christ as the Bishop of the world on its eastern side. A little wish hole in the cross usually has a couple of coppers left there, and if you want to say a prayer or whatever you are continuing a tradition at least 800 years old. From the cross take the track east between the dry stone walls back to the castle and your car.

ROUTE 22
MILLTOWN MALBAY AND SPANISH POINT

Map: OS Discovery Series Map No. 57
Distance: 7km
Grade: Easy
Average time: 2-3 hrs
Getting there from Ennis: Less than 50m on the southern side of the N85/N18 roundabout in Ennis take the R474 road west towards Milltown Malbay. This will take you past the golf course. Continue along this road through the village of Connolly after about 14 km where you veer left, staying on the R474. Pass through the Hands Cross Roads after a further 5km with a telephone kiosk for identification purposes. 6km from the Hands Cross Roads veer gently right, and continue here in a straight line to Milltown Malbay.
Parking: Park in the village.
Starting point: Irish National Grid reference R055790

One of the busiest times to visit Milltown Malbay is during the Willie Clancy Festival, when you can brush shoulders with all the stars of Irish traditional and folk music. The concert in the town hall is a great event, which should not be missed, if at all possible.

Leave Milltown Malbay and take the main road, the N67, south towards Kilkee and Kilrush. There is a footpath all along this section of road which makes

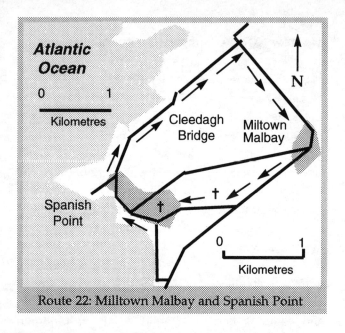

Route 22: Milltown Malbay and Spanish Point

life very easy. Continue past the holiday homes on your left and right, with hints of the ocean off to your right. After 1.5km a road to your right signposted to Spanish Point should be taken. You will pass the Anglican Church on your right, with its bright red roof and unusual spire. You will shortly arrive into Spanish Point. There is a lovely view west and a walk along the beach is a must. A visit during an Atlantic storm is equally rewarding, as 5,000km of Atlantic ocean attempts to dump itself into a tiny harbour.

Follow the main road, the R482, around past the hotel on your left, and out of Spanish Point along the coast northwards with the ocean on your left-hand side. In a storm the little cove to your left at Cleedagh Bridge is even more impressive than Spanish Point, but do take care as the ocean is very unpredictable. Walk northwards along the road from here back to the main road at a T-junction. Keep an eye out for cars coming around the sharp bend to your left, and turn right heading back into Milltown Malbay, which appears to be a lot nearer than it is.

ROUTE 23
THE CASTLE OF DROMORE AND DROMORE WOOD

Maps: OS Discovery Series Maps No. 57 and 58
Distance: 3km
Grade: Easy
Average time: 45 minutes
Getting there from Ennis: Leave Ennis by the N85, which branches off the N18 at the roundabout at the northern end of the town. After approximately 4km go right on to the R476 at Fountain Crossroads. This road leads towards Corrofin. After 6km you come to a sign for Dysert O'Dea Archaeology Centre to your left, but go down the side road opposite to the east. After 1km you come to the first of three T-junctions and go left here. Almost immediately this takes you around a sharp bend to your right. Continue down the hill to the next T-junction and go right. After 2km a bend going right has a small road leading off it to the north. This is the third junction, and you go right southwards towards Ruan, now on map No. 58. 300m away the road bends left at Tullyodea and at the end of the bend go straight on along the narrow road eastwards. Go along this road through a crossroads after 1km. Continue along for another 2km until you reach Dromore Wood.
Parking: Turn right and drive into the parking area.
Starting point: Irish National Grid Reference R354865

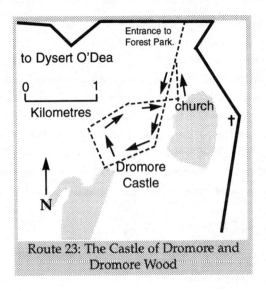

Entrance to
Forest Park.

to Dysert O'Dea

0   1

Kilometres

church

Dromore
Castle

N

Route 23: The Castle of Dromore and
Dromore Wood

From the parking area go west to 'the Castle of Dromore' made famous by the song of the same name lamenting the destruction of the Gaelic order by the English invasions. The site of the castle is spectacular, on the point of the lake with a lovely view to the south. Continue along the track west past the castle, and this brings you around in a circle back on to the main track in the wood after 1km. You are walking through some of the remaining original oak, holly, and birch woods which are the natural woodland for the island. It is said that a squirrel could go from one end of Munster to the other without ever touching the ground such was the extent of the forest. Most of County Clare was covered by this forest until the sixteenth century when it was chopped down for use in smelters, mines and British Navy ships.

Once you reach the main track pick your way eastwards through the woods to the second of the Dromore lakes. Following the waters edge northwards you will come to the old church 100m away, associated with Dromore castle, which is also worth a look. From this a track leads northwards to the main forest road and once you reach this, you go left southwards back to the carpark and your car.

ROUTE 24
BUNRATTY CASTLE

Map: OS Discovery Series Map No. 58
Distance: 5km
Grade: Easy
Average time: 1-2 hrs
Getting there from Limerick: Leave Limerick, and head west towards Ennis on the N18. After 9km take the slip road for Bunratty, and go right over the bridge across the dual-carriageway. At the T-junction go right into the village, and past one of Ireland's most famous castles. Park in the carpark of Durty Nellie's pub in the shadow of the castle.
Starting point: Irish National Grid Reference R450610
Cross the old humpback bridge towards the castle. Go right, northwards along the riverbank. Continue up this road and out into open countryside. You pass a large number of fine modern houses and bungalows. This road reaches the main Sixmilebridge to Shannon road (R471) after 2km at a T-junction. Go left here towards Shannon.

After 500m you come to a crossroads and you go left here towards Bunratty. The road rises gently until you reach the summit of Bunratty hill. Here in 1310, yet another of the many battles between O'Brien factions was fought over succession rights. Normans from Galway fought against Normans from Limerick as a result of family commitments.

The view from the hill is particularly splendid

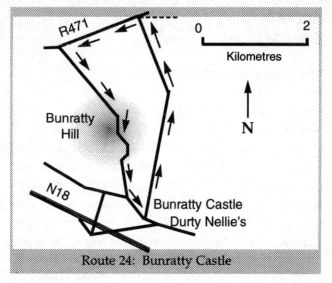

Route 24: Bunratty Castle

dominating some of the best land in Munster, while to the west is Shannon town. This town was built in the 1950s and 1960s to service the airport and duty free zone, a concept invented here. Plane buffs will enjoy watching the jets take off and land, and the main approach is pretty much over this hill. The view south is breathtaking with a magnificent panorama over the Shannon estuary. From here continue directly down the hill to the village, and turn left, eastwards, back towards the castle. If you have time a visit to the Bunratty Folk Park is recommended, as is a visit to Durty Nellie's pub.

ROUTE 25
LOOP HEAD

Map: OS Discovery Map No. 63
Distance: 12km
Grade: Easy
Average time: 3-4 hrs
Getting there from Ennis: Leave Ennis on the N68. Head to Kilrush 42 km away. In Kilrush go right up the hill and follow the signs for Kilkee on to the N67. At Kilkee go left at the beach. Continue out of the town on the R487 up the hill past the Church towards Carrigaholt and Loop Head. After 7km the road takes a sharp left and there is a junction to your right for Loop Head. Go right at the junction and continue through Cross village reached after 5km. 3km beyond the village the road takes a sharpish left with a minor road going straight on. Go straight on towards Ross reached after 3km.
Parking: Once in Ross go right to park in the carpark.
Starting point: Irish National Grid Reference Q734503

Loop Head is an elongated peninsula, which sticks out of County Clare and provides wonderful views of County Kerry, the Shannon estuary, Clare, the Aran Islands and even Galway. It is one of the places that any visitor to Clare should get to at some stage.

From Ross carpark walk back down the road towards the road for Loop Head. Once you reach this,

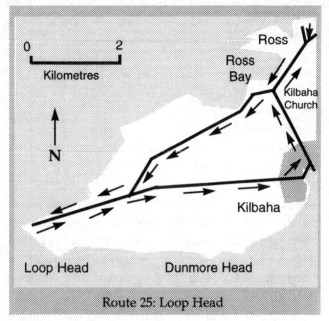

Route 25: Loop Head

go right westwards towards Loop Head. Walk down the hill passing Ross Bay on you right. After 600m you come to a junction. Ahead of you and to the left at the top of the hill is Kilbaha church, but you take the road to the right.

Wander down this to the coast on your right after 300m and continue westwards uphill. You reach the top of the hill after 1.5km and there is a fine view over the Atlantic. Once you reach the junction with the R487 at the top of the hill go right towards Loop Head, which is 1.5km to the west. Loop Head has always had a lighthouse on it and it is no surprise to find one there today. Continue past the lighthouse towards the headland with care.

Off to your right is Diarmuid and Gráinne's island. Gráinne was betrothed to Finn MacCumhail, head of Ireland's legendary warriors the Fianna, in his old age and was less than happy. She put Diarmuid O'Duibhne (a young member of the Fianna) under obligation to assist her escape, and thus began one of the great epic chases. Matters were finally resolved with Gráinne getting her way, and going off with Diarmuid to live in Corca Dhuibhne (Dingle), the peninsula that still bears the family name. Sadly, Diarmuid was gored by a boar, and Finn refused to use his magic powers to save the young man's life. The story at Loop Head is that the pair leapt across to the island for a night's sleep to avoid Finn. In fact, even in the 1820s, the headland was known as Leap Head, and only got corrupted in recent times. At least in Irish the headland retains its original name. The view from here is excellent, all the way from the Dingle peninsula north to the Aran Islands.

After your visit return along the main road, R487, back up the hill towards Kilbaha, 5km away. Take the road to your left, just before the Post Office, and continue uphill past first the school and then the church on your left. Continue northwards from the church and at the next junction go right past Ross Bay back to your car by the castle.

ROUTE 26
NEWMARKET ON FERGUS, QUIN AND DROMOLAND CASTLE

Map: OS Discovery Map No. 58
Distance: 18km
Grade: Moderate
Average time: 5.5-6.5 hrs
Getting there from Ennis: Head south on the N18 through Clarecastle with its sharp left. Pass the castle on your left and the chemical factory on your right. Continue right around the bend and continue for 8km to Newmarket on Fergus.
Parking: Park in the town.
Starting point: Irish National Grid reference R396680

The first section of this walk follows the Mid Clare Way to Quin, the heartland of Clare hurling. The N18 takes a sharp left in Newmarket and goes sharp right almost immediately. However, you walk east down the main street along the R470. At the end of the built-up area take the left fork up the minor road away from the water tower. A few metres later go left again, heading north. After 2km from the start you pass one of the many O'Brien tower houses that you will encounter on this walk. 200m beyond the castle you come to a T-junction and go right here. Continue around a bend to your right and then left as you enter the conifer plantation. At the carpark on your left,

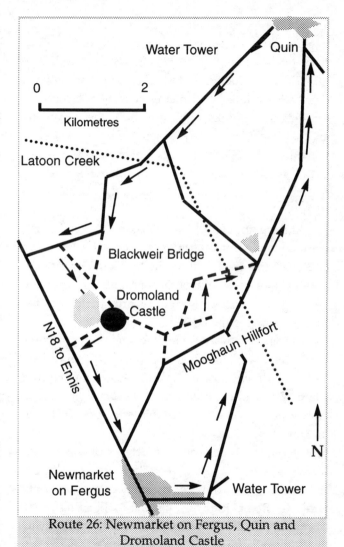

Water Tower

Quin

0   2

Kilometres

Latoon Creek

Blackweir Bridge

Dromoland
Castle

N18 to Ennis

Mooghaun Hillfort

Newmarket
on Fergus

Water Tower

N

**Route 26: Newmarket on Fergus, Quin and
Dromoland Castle**

leave the minor road and follow a track through the trees. A couple of metres down this track take a detour right to Mooghaun hillfort which is very well preserved despite being almost 2,500 years old. Where this leads left after a few metres go right and continue through the conifers until you reach the stream by another tower house on your left. Go right and follow the track by the stream back down onto the minor road opposite Lough Ataska which is straight ahead of you. Turn left northwards here and walk along the road to the next bend.

At the point of the bend in Kilkieran go right eastwards down a track past two old houses. After 300m you leave this track and go right on a track that goes under the Limerick-Ennis railway line. Just after you go under the line, go left northwards parallel to the railway down to the Burren.

Go right eastwards along the road until you come to a T-junction. Go left here and walk into Quin 1.5km away. You have now completed stage 1 of the Mid Clare Way and a visit to one of the finest Franciscan Abbeys in Ireland is a must. Quin Abbey can be found on your right halfway up the main street and the gravestones will tell you as much about the area as anything else.

Leave Quin, with the water tower on your right and the River Rine on your left, heading west. Continue down this road for 3km under the railway line. After 3km the road takes a sharp left. Follow this until the road turns to the right at Blackweir Bridge. Cross the bridge and continue as far as the side entance to the Dromoland Castle Estate which is the second junction on your left. Continue through the grounds of the five-star hotel and treat yourself to afternoon tea.

Take any road or track south to return to Newmaket on Fergus, 1km away.

ROUTE 27
DÚN AONGHASA ON THE ARAN ISLANDS

Map: OS Discovery Series Map No. 51
Distance: 14km
Grade: Moderate
Average time: 3.5-4.5 hrs
Getting there from Galway: Get a ferry from Galway City or Rossaveal, or, get an Aer Aran flight from Rossaveal.
Starting point: Irish National Grid reference L883090

During the summer season the islands can barely cope with the visitors and it is much more fun to go in the winter, during a storm! Try to stay overnight and be prepared to stay a little longer if there is bad weather.

Dún Aonghasa is the jewel in the crown of the Aran Islands. Built at least 3,000 years ago, it stands at the top of a 90m cliff which falls directly to the Atlantic. Three outer rings of stones defended the inhabitants from attack, but huge questions are always asked about it. First, the islands are miles from the nearest land, so why did the builders need such massive defences, when even getting to the island was a major undertaking. Second, why does the open side-face into the sea and the prevailing wind; did some of the fort fall into the sea in the intervening years. Third, with no water supply, how were the defenders

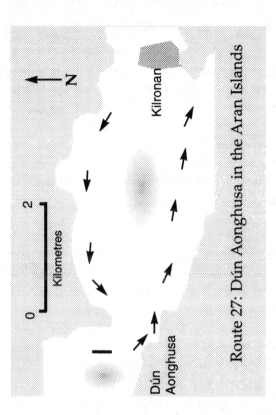

Route 27: Dún Aonghusa in the Aran Islands

going to survive a siege of more than a couple of days? Finally, given the massive labour required, how and why was it organised at the western edge of Europe at a time when there was no known civilisation to the west?

From Kilronan head out the main road on the Island towards Eochaill and Cill Mhuirbhigh. This takes you past the ruined church on your right. If you are there in the summer, visit the Heritage Centre to see the film *Man of Aran*. After 5km you come to Port Mhuirbhigh on your right-hand side, with its lovely sandy beach. From the beach continue into Cill Mhuirbhigh, and go left here at the old churches. A sign for Dún Aonghasa will direct you down the track towards the fort, which is 1km away. Walk up to the fort through the *cheveaux de frise* (outer defensive ring of pointed stones) and through the entrance. The sudden drop ahead is quite unnerving, so take care.

From the fort walk eastwards along the cliff edge for 1km around Blind Sound, and up to Poll na bPéist. This is a block plucked out of the limestone pavement to form a natural swimming hole. From here follow the track eastwards (little walking-men to help you) back to the road at Gort na gCapall. Go right eastwards along the boreen, and after 1.5km you pass a junction to your left on the way-marked trail. Go straight on eastwards here for 600m until you come to the second track on your left. If you are a peak-bagger you will simply have to go left here up to Dún Eochla, the highest point on the island. This also has an old lighthouse to confirm its position. Continue northwards to the road and turn right here eastwards along the main road back to Kilronan.

If you are not a peak-bagger continue east instead of turning left for 2.5km until you reach An Poll Mór beach. Go left here northwards back into Kilronan just around the bay from the beach.

ROUTE 28
GLEANN NA NDEOR ON THE ARAN ISLANDS

Map: OS Discovery Series Map No. 51
Distance: 10km
Grade: Easy
Average time: 2.5-3.5 hrs
Getting there from Galway: Get a ferry from Galway city or Rossaveal. Get an Aer Aran flight from Rossaveal.
Starting point: Irish National Grid reference L883090

From Kilronan walk southwards towards Cill Éinne passing An Poll Mór beach on you left after 1km. Just beyond this on your right is Loch an tSáile, and 1km beyond this you will reach Cill Éinne. On you left is the airstrip, and continue past the old church and round tower towards the entrance to the Airport. As the road swings left into the Airport take a sharp right down a marked track towards Iaráirne, and after 1km this track goes left after passing through the houses in Iaráirne.

Go straight on here on the marked track and after 200m go right, southwards, uphill towards Aill na nGlasóg. This has a fine view of Inis Meáinn. On the right day the blow-holes to your right will put on a spectacular performance as the force of the Atlantic is squeezed through the narrow fissures in the rock underneath, and out through the top of the holes. Reverse your route back to Kilronan.

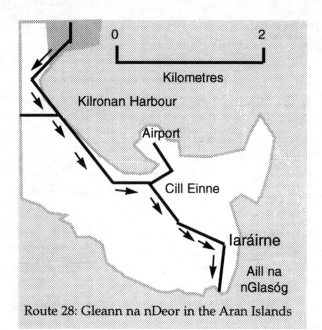

0　　　　　　　　　　　　2
Kilometres
Kilronan Harbour
Airport
Cill Einne
Iaráirne
Aill na nGlasóg
Route 28: Gleann na nDeor in the Aran Islands

106

Route 29
The Burren Way (BW)

Maps: OS Discovery Series Maps No. 57 and No. 51
Distance: 30km
Grade: Very difficult
Average time: 2 days
Getting there from Ennis: Take the N85 which branches off the N18 at the roundabout at the northern end of Ennis. Follow this road until you reach Ennistimon after 24km. Take the first left in Ennistimon on to the N67 and go west to Lehinch 2km away. At Lehinch go right at the Garda Station and north along the R478 Liscannor road past the golf links on your left. A sharp left at O'Briens Bridge will bring you to Liscannor, 4km from Lehinch.
Parking: Park anywhere on the main street
Starting point: Irish National Grid reference R065883

Day 1: Follow route 2 as far as the visitor centre on the Burren Way. From the visitor centre go north along the road towards Doolin. 1km later the road takes a sharp left and then right. Continue down the road for another kilometre and the BW goes left off the road before swinging northwards again to rejoin the road after another kilometre. Walk down the boreen to Fisher Street/Doolin where you should stay for the night. This is one of the centres of Irish traditional music, and you can while away the happy evening hours. If you are lucky any one of Ireland's best musicians may be present playing for fun, which is an experience not easily forgotten.

Day 2: Walk 1km back to the main road, R479. Cross the Aille river and continue along past the Post Office towards the church on your right. Right underneath you is one of the largest stalactites in the world which is part of the Doolin cave system. As yet only experienced cavers can view this marvel but there are plans to open a show-cave. The cave actually extends under the river which is highly unusual in limestone as it would be expected that the joints and fissures in the rock would have caused the river to have broken through to the cave underneath. 4km up the road you come to Ballynalacken Castle and hotel in the old O'Brien seat (Route 6). Continue along the BW and join the Green Road (Route 7) above Fanore which cuts across the limestone under the hump of Slieve Elva to your right. This 2.5km section is quite easy as the ground is flat. The views out to your left over the sea are very good. The track turns eastwards, and downhill steeply enough into the Caher River valley.

Pass a couple of old houses on your left and you reach the tarred road 1km from where you started to descend the hill. On the tarred road go left downhill over the bridge to the crossroads. Follow the signs for the Burren Way. These bring you steeply uphill over a ridge and down the other side to a track reached after

1.5km. Go right at the T-junction and walk down the side of the Rathborney River. You are heading southwards. After 2km the road follows the river sharp left and continues eastwards to the main road, N67, through the Burren. The BW goes left down a narrow road at this junction and follow this. After 1km you pass a tower house on your right called Newtown Castle. Continue straight on for 2km down to the coast and go right on the R477. Walk along the road into Ballyvaghan. Now all you have to do is walk back to your car 30km away!

Route 30
The East Clare Way (ECW)

Maps: OS Discovery Series Maps No. 58 and 52
Distance: 121km
Grade: Very difficult
Average time: 6-7 days
Getting there: Start at Killaloe at the southern end of Lough Derg.
Starting point: Irish National Grid reference R700730

Day 1
Distance: 17km
Average time: 5-6 hrs
Killaloe to Broadford
The normal way to do the East Clare Way is the reverse of this walk, but by doing it this way you keep some of the best views to last. It is really up to yourself.

From Killaloe take the ECW west out of the town on the small road between the Garda Station on your left and the church on your right. Continue out of the town past the garages on your right uphill. In the fields on your left are a couple of standing stones which are worth a look if you wish. After 2km you come to a crossroads just after a side road to your left, signposted ,and you go left down the road southwards for 1.5km to the next crossroads. There is a lovely old church on your left at the crossroads.

Go right up the hill westwards, steeply enough at

first, and follow the road along the side of the Ardcloony River valley towards the col between Lackareagh Mountain and Glenvagalliagh Mountain, 4km ahead. You reach the col staying on the road, and there is a lovely view of the central part of Clare as you come out of the woods. Drop down the hill westward to Kilbane.

Go right uphill past the school, and after 1km you come to a junction on the right with a sign for the ECW. Go up this road and follow the little walking man signs out on to the open mountainside. You go left at the end of the track, over a stream and across the mountainside for 1.5km to another minor road just above a sharp hairpin bend. This is signposted. Continue up this track through the wood to a left turn, and down the other side to a T-junction beside Drimmeen wood on your right. Go left here 1km into Broadford where you should have accommodation arranged.

Day 2

Distance: 26km

Average time: 7-8 hrs

Broadford to Tulla

Head south from Broadford on the Limerick road, R465, past the O'Briensbridge junction on your left, and take the ECW right at the next Y-junction at Gortnagogh. This is signposted. Follow this for 800m, and go left for 400m to an old house. Go right here along the ECW track and you come to a road after 1km. Continue along this uphill for 300m, and take another signed ECW track to your right just before the wood. Follow this along and take all signs through the wood that keep you on the ECW through to Knockshanvo.

This leads you to another minor road after 3km, where the ECW takes a turn northwards. This is short-ly followed by a sharp left westwards. Follow this down the hill going right at the next junction with the tarred road. At the next T-junction go left and over the Ahaclare River. Just after the river the ECW goes right but by going straight on here you can cut off a fairly pointless section of the Way.

After 1km you pass through Cappalahee Cross Roads and continue straight. After 1.5km you come to another one and go straight through here. 250m ahead you rejoin the ECW (coming in from your right) at Cappalaheen Bridge just as you enter the woods. Continue through the woods. At the main road, R462, 1.5km away, go right and then sharp left westwards. This takes you past Lough Cullaunyheeda on you left after 700m. At the end of the lake go left once you enter the wood and south along the ECW track. At the end of the woods you visit Craggaunowen, before turning north.

Cross the main road, R352, after 3km and contin-ue along the ECW until you swing around into Tulla where you should stay for the night.

DAY 3
Distance: 19km
Average time: 6-7 hrs
Tulla to Lough Graney

Leave Tulla on the R462 leading towards Gort. Just
before the end of the village take the minor road to
your right. Continue up this as it goes left around a
gentle bend after 1km.

At the Y-junction beyond the bend go straight on
following the ECW signs. 1km down this from the
junction you pass Cloondooney Lough on your right.
You join the main road, R462, 200m beyond this and
go right. This is all drumlin country with large glacial
deposits dumped in the form of low hills with poor
drainage between. Once past the low hill of
Drumullan go left off the main road heading west.
After 1km you cross a stream and pass a few houses
on your left. Just beyond the houses a lane leads into
a farmhouse on your right. Pass this, then a few houses on your left and after 200m you go sharp right
northwards at the junction. This brings you uphill into
the foothills of Maghera with its TV transmitter on the
summit to guide your way.

You drop down into the upper reaches of the
Affick River and cross the stream by another set of
houses on your left. The ground rises to a crossroads
with the ECW going straight by Affick. Continue up
the hill which rises fairly steeply up into the trees. The

road reaches a T-junction with the road going left and a track leading right eastwards across the face of the hill. This is the ECW and waymarked. Follow this track over the hill and down into the upper reaches of the Annagapple River. Continue along eastwards around the other side of the valley by Uggoon Upper. You cross another track and, 200m beyond this, the ECW goes sharp left northwards along the side of Glenaree River valley. The track rises gently through the trees for 1km and you go right to reach the access road leading to Lough Ea. Walk up this road around the bend to your right and gently along to the next bend to the left 1km away. You depart the access track just around the bend and head east across the boggy ground above the couple of lakes below you.

After 1.5km you reach another tarred road on the point of the ridge. This road runs north-south and you reach it just above a zig-zag in the road. The ECW way goes broadly straight on but you are much better off going left northwards downhill along the road to eliminate some of the rough ground. Continue down the road past the access road for Maghera reached after 1.25km. 700m beyond the Maghera entrance you come to a junction to your right. The ECW rejoins your route here but 100m later it goes off to the left at a Y-junction. Continue straight on and 1.5km later you reach a T-junction. You have now reached the main Feakle-Gort road, R461, and go left northwards towards Lough Graney. 300m later the main road goes

114

left around a bend and you take the minor road into Caher 700m away by the lake. There may be problems getting accommodation hereabouts so make sure of this in advance.

DAY 4
Distance: 18.5km
Average time: 5-6 hrs
Easy Circuit of Lough Graney to Flagmount - optional

Follow Route 14

DAY 5
Distance: 20km
Average time: 5.5-6.5 hrs
Lough Graney to Mountshannon
Leave Caher heading east to Bunshoon Bridge. Just past the school you come to a junction with a sign for the ECW going straight on and a sign for Feakle point-ing back the way you came. Go left here and walk along the road with good views of Lough Graney to your left. 2km up this road you reach the village of Flagmount. Just beyond the church is a sign pointing up a lane for the ECW. Up you go. Once you reach the side road after a fairly steep climb, go left. Follow the side road around the bend and go right at the Y-junc-tion uphill. Pass yet another stand of conifers on your right and take a slight detour west here for 300m for a fine view down over the lake.

Go back to the track and turn right southwards,

downhill. At the next junction go left eastwards past the megalithic tomb along the side of the mountain, and around the valley. At the T-junction reached after 1.25km go left up around the bend to your right past a junction going left onto the summit of Knockbeha. 400m beyond this junction the ECW goes right through the trees southwards uphill to Corrakyle and onto the ridge. If you feel like it you can walk along the top of the ridge, but the ECW goes down the track to the minor road south of you. Once you reach this after 700m go left eastwards past the old graveyard on your right. After 1km the road bends right where another track comes in from your left. Go southwards along the side of the glen and left at the next Y-junction after 200m. Continue along this track for 5km as it undulates just under the line of the ridge.

Ahead of you to the left is Scalp mountain hidden behind the trees. After 5km you cross Turkenagh Bridge over the upper reaches of the Corra River just under the col between the two hills. The road rises to cross the ridge ahead and then drops down southwards over the upper reaches of the Bow River. Just beyond this the ECW goes left uphill, but in reality this is the start of a long, involved and somewhat pointless detour which is best avoided.

Continue south along the road you are on, along the side of the river valley. You rejoin the ECW (this is not marked on Map 52), and continue to a bend by a stand of conifers where the road goes eastwards over the ridge to your left. Follow this into Mountshannon. This is a lovely village to stay in and is even a Tidy Towns winner. You also get an opportunity for a visit and guided tour of Holy Island with its ancient monastic settlement while in the village.

DAY 6
Mountshannon to Killaloe
Distance: 17km
Average time: 7-8 hrs
The normal way to do the East Clare Way is the reverse of this walk, but by doing it this way you keep some of the best views to last. It is really up to yourself.

Today we pretty much leave the ECW behind for much of the walk to Scarriff. Leave Mountshannon by the main road R352 heading towards Scarriff past the church on your left. 200m beyond this the main road bends left and you go right at the junction up the minor road to Woodpark Bridge. The road you are on is as straight as an Irish road gets and continue along it for 3.5km until you reach the Bow River. On your way you pass Woodpark Demesne on your left which is one of the many big houses in the area. At the Bow River go left over the bridge. Continue down this road and away from the river bank. After 1km you come to another of those crossroads, where the roads coming in from your right and left don't quite meet. Continue through this somewhat complicated junction, and over Ballyboy Bridge heading southwest towards

Scarriff which you reach after 2km.

The most noticeable thing about Scarriff is the smell from the timber factory and this tends to stop people from resting here. Continue along the R352 to Tuamgraney 1km to the south. Here you should visit the Heritage Centre and the oldest church in Ireland still in use. Continue south out of the town on the Killaloe road R463. Where this bends left at the end of the houses, the ECW goes right uphill. This is sign-posted.

Go up the side road going right at the first junction after 500m and left at the second junction through the trees uphill a further 500m on. This brings you after 2km to a T-junction, and go left uphill towards the trees.

You come to a crossroads 600m ahead. Go left towards Caherhurly National School about 300 metres away. You cross this via Knocknalecka and the road swings around descending across the face of the ridge. You are now 4.5km from Caherhurly School. The ECW goes right eastwards downhill as it weaves back and forth to a T-junction at Drehidbower Bridge. Go right here and continue to a bridge over the Annacarriga River. 200m beyond the bridge the East Clare Way goes left westwards uphill. Go straight on here over another stream, and 200m later you reach the main Killaloe Road R463. Go right here, southwards and into Killaloe 3.5km away for rest and recreation.

NEW IRISH WALKS AND SCRAMBLES

Barry Keane

The walks described in these books vary from pleasant strolls to more strenuous scrambles. Most of these have not featured in previous guidebooks and so provide a range of new options.

1. THE IVERAGH PENINSULA
£5.99 PB   *1 898256 27 6*

2. THE DINGLE PENINSULA
£5.99 PB   *1 898256 28 4*

3. THE BEARA AND MIZEN HEAD PENINSULAS
£5.99 PB   *1 898256 29 2*

4. THE GALTY, KNOCKMEALDOWN AND COMERAGH MOUNTAINS
£5.99 PB   *1 898256 48 9*

5. THE BURREN, ARAN ISLANDS AND COUNTY CLARE
£6.99 PB   *1 898256 83 7*

and by
Joe Cronin

6. RAMBLES IN CORK CITY AND COUNTY
£7.99 PB   *1 898256 72 1*

WILD PLANTS OF THE BURREN AND ARAN ISLANDS

Charles E. Nelson

The Burren and Aran Islands are renowned worldwide for the beauty of their natural flora. In this book, Charles Nelson has selected 120 of the most widely occurring plus a number of special plants. Introduced by short chapters giving background information on the plants and instructions on how to use the guide, photographs are grouped according to flower colour and the pages are colour coded. Plants are described simply using the common English name, followed by the name in Irish and then the Latin (botanical) name. The flowering period and each plant's distribution are given succinctly.

£10.00 PB   *1 898256 70 5*

THE WAY THAT I WENT

Robert Lloyd Praeger

Written by Ireland's greatest field botanist and first published in 1937, this book crackles with the excitement and perplexity aroused by our then heritage of tombs and ring forts.

With a major new introduction by writer, Michael Viney, putting the book in context, it relates it to contemporary issues such as conservation, ecology and farming practices.

£11.99 PB   *1 898256 35 7*